Day Services for People with Learning Disabilities

of related interest

Handbook for Assessing and Managing Care in the Community
Philip Seed and Gillian Kaye
ISBN 1 85302 227 6

Introducing Network Analysis in Social Work
Philip Seed
ISBN 1 85302 034 6 hb
ISBN 1 85302 106 7 pb

Is Day Care Still at the Crossroads?
Philip Seed
ISBN 1 85302 373 6

Social Work in the Wake of Disasters
David Tumelty
ISBN 1 85302 060 5

Day Services for People with Learning Disabilities

Philip Seed

Jessica Kingsley Publishers
London and Bristol, Pennsylvania

First published in the United Kingdom in 1996 by
Jessica Kingsley Publishers Ltd
116 Pentonville Road
London N1 9JB, England
and
1900 Frost Road, Suite 101
Bristol, PA 19007, U S A

Library of Congress Cataloging in Publication Data
Day services for people with learning disabilities / edited by Philip Seed.
p. cm. – (Case studies for practice : 7)
Includes bibliographical references and index.
ISBN 1-85302-339-6 (alk. paper)
1. Day care centers for the mentally handicapped. 2. Mentally handicapped–Services for. 3. Learning disabled–Services for,
I. Seed, Philip. II. Series.
HV3004.D38 1996
362.3'83–dc20 96-41380
CIP

British Library Cataloguing in Publication Data
Day services for people with Learning Disabilities. – (Case studies for Practice; No.7)
I. Seed, Philip II. Series
362.282

ISBN 1-85302-339-6

Printed and Bound in Great Britain by
Cromwell Press Ltd., Melksham

Contents

Figures

Preface

This book updates and replaces three books published in the *Case Studies for Practice* series, now out of print, namely:

Day Services for People with Mental Handicaps

Day Services for People with Severe Handicaps

Towards Independent Living

The new book stands alone with more space devoted to background discussion of the different issues raised in the case studies. The studies themselves are restricted to people with learning disabilities attending day services. Material relating to other client groups is not included.

The original studies were undertaken ten years ago. They have been updated so that we have a rare opportunity to review what has happened to people attending day services over a ten-year period.

Points for Discussion have been updated and are listed after each case, or group of cases, as in the original volumes.

The book is addressed to staff, trainee staff and students working with people with learning disabilities. It may also interest parents and other carers.

The studies may be helpful in conjunction with professional training, in-service training and distance learning. They may be used to supplement other training materials. Some of these materials are included in a list for further reading.

I am grateful to all who have helped in the reproduction and revision of the material, especially the people whose stories are told and who gave permission for their experiences to be written about in order to assist staff training. Their names are fictitious. Where they live and the names of the centres they attend are not disclosed. In other respects, the material is authentic.

I am also grateful to my colleagues who helped in the production of the original books or in the present revision and updating – especially Margaret Thomson and Fiona Harkess.

Philip Seed
University of Dundee
Department of Social Work
May 1995

CHAPTER ONE

Developments in Day Services During the Past Ten Years

The people whose lives are described in this book originally formed part of a random sample of 146 cases studied in 15 representative centres in different parts of Scotland between 1984 and 1986. A full report of the research was published in *Day Care at the Cross-Roads* (Seed 1988). A shorter revised version has since been produced for training purposes (Seed 1996).

To answer the question: 'What has happened since?' is, strictly speaking, that we do not know. No further research on the scale and depth of *Day Care at the Cross-Roads* has been funded. However, the exercise required to update *Case Studies for Practice* for this volume provides some glimpses and illustrations of changes in the past ten years. These, together with other smaller research and evaluation projects in which the author and others have been involved suggest the following changes and trends.

Day service provision for people with learning disabilities has continued, if more slowly, to expand.

Some of the worst buildings have been replaced or are planned to be replaced.

The role of the voluntary sector has changed. Some voluntary projects which were pioneering services 10–20 years ago have been taken over by local authorities. However, other more recent voluntary sector initiatives have taken their place, often concentrating on more specialist needs for specific client groups such as people with autism, cerebral palsy, profound learning disabilities. As is traditional, parents and parent-based organisations have played a key role.

The private sector has been slow to develop initiatives in day care but this may change.

More generally, day services have taken advantage of the 'enterprise culture'. It is easier for day services to move from traditional activities to the kinds of enterprises and projects that give 'clients' of services other roles: for example, as staff helping to run cafés, shops or other small business enterprises.

Specific projects preparing people for employment have continued to develop. Perhaps this has not been on the scale one would have liked, bearing in mind the continued relatively high levels of unemployment. European Community funding is being used in some instances.

Links with further education colleges do not appear to have developed as much as might have been expected in the light of initiatives ten years ago. The aims and policies of these colleges is currently being studied both in England and Wales (Tomlinson) and in Scotland (Thomson).

There have been radical changes during the past ten years in thinking about supported accommodation in place of traditional residential establishments. Many traditional residential establishments remain, especially in the private sector. How far day services fit in, or have responded to opportunities to prepare their clients for more independent living varies – as the case studies in this volume illustrate.

Changes in day service staff roles were apparent during the 1984–6 studies. More day service staff are now trained – though the variety of the parameters or what may be considered appropriate training and qualifications remains.

In general, activities at centres or from centres have become more purposeful. The worst passive drifting, or in some cases eccentricities, of practice have – at least on the basis of the current updating of the cases for this book – ceased in favour of more regularised and purposeful assessment and individualised programme planning, with key workers in place.

The movement towards activities in the community, using the centre as a base and a resource rather than as the place where people attend to undertake activities has continued unevenly. The centre described in Chapter 7 (the example of William) has moved along this road, for example. Some centres (notably the centre described in Chapter 8) already had part-time attendance as the norm in the 1980s.

It is less clear – and should be researched – how far centre programmes are integrated with effective holistic care in the community plans. However, local authority care plans do seem to have more substance, and maybe a little less rhetoric, compared with ten years ago. It is often claimed that financial constraints have tended to restrict staffing which is required to implement more individualised care plans. There is scope for research to test how far this is the case.

Whatever the staffing constraints, there are opportunities to improve practice. The case studies in this volume are presented in the context of learning from what has happened in the past to be better able to realise what is possible now and in the future, even within current financial restraints.

CHAPTER TWO

Some Key Practice Issues

1. CARE IN THE COMMUNITY – INTEGRATION OR SEGREGATION

Care in the community has had major implications for day services for people with learning disabilities. Day services are part of a total care provision for the individual client. This care plan is based on an holistic assessment of client needs in the context of their home and community background.

Day services are now expected to be provided on a commissioned basis. This means they are costed and purchased after a process of assessment, care planning and service review.

Day services are services provided *in the community*. This means, amongst other things, that they are a means to enable people with learning disabilities to become more integrated in what is going on around them in the community – in terms of people, places and activities – and not segregated.

Integration is a means to a better quality of life. This is a general goal and an aspiration which people with learning disabilities share with the rest of us. Quality of life provides a set of criteria for measuring the benefits of human services as a whole.

These points embody the ideals intended in the care in the community legislation of 1993 and in the discussions that have accompanied its implementation. In practice there will be shortcomings and difficulties. But we need to have the ideals, goals and values clear as starting points for discussing practice.

What does 'integration' mean? A few years ago it was popular to suggest that day services were a form of segregation. By attending a day service, people were kept from taking part in more normal activities in the community, in 'ordinary' places (like community centres, colleges, work places etc.). This need not be so. Day services can serve as gateways to opportunities in employment, moving to more independent living, and leisure and friendships with people in the community. Day services can assess and respond to support needs to fulfil these opportunities. Integration means real involvement based on personal choice in meeting and getting to know new people, visiting new places and exploring potential through new activities.

The case studies focus on how far these goals are achieved.

2. EDUCATIONAL GOALS OR CONTAINMENT

Day services can serve one of two broad functions:

(a) They can educate, train and support people in developing potential and realising opportunities, looking to the future. They can help families adjust to changing life circumstances. They can prepare the way for people to leave home, as adults, with whatever appropriate support and care are needed. They can support people who have left long-stay hospitals to adjust to the new opportunities living in the community can offer. This is the positive option.

(b) The negative option is to use day services to contain an existing lifestyle and structure and offer little more than this. Attendance at a centre can enable the parents or other carers just to carry on. The person with a disability remains the family 'child'. The family structure in itself may be beneficial – there may be opportunities within it for enjoyment, caring, varied activities and so on. Sometimes this may not be the case. Opportunities may be very limited. Whether beneficial or not, circumstances will bring about changes. Family and other support structures *must* change. Parents have to think about the future when they can no longer manage. People with disabilities themselves may want to leave home and even if they do not say so they may act out their feelings of restlessness. In the past, people with learning disabilities might be offered places in long-stay hospitals when parents could not cope and there containment continued. This option is no longer acceptable or possible.

Containment, then, is no longer a basis for offering a day service. The future of day services lies in developing the positive option.

The case studies demonstrate where these alternative policies have led in terms of the quality of life and quality of care for those concerned.

3. RESPITE

Relief or respite for carers is important. It remains a major function of day services to provide a break, both to carers and to people with disabilities, from being in one another's way or in making too great demands on one another. This is especially important in cases where:

- There is a single parent.
- Parents are at work.
- The person has a severe disability.
- There is more than one member of the household with a disability.
- Parents or other carers are elderly.
- Parents have conflicting demands in caring for different people in the family household.

Respite can be provided in many different ways and often more than one way is required. For example, weekend breaks may supplement the weekday relief which a regular day service can provide. A few specialist day services now provide weekend or evening respite as well as a day service.

However, respite by itself is not the main aim of a day service. Respite is secondary to the educational thrust of maximising opportunities, developing potential and preparing for the future.

Chapter 6 explores these issues in detail.

4. ELDERLY PEOPLE WITH DISABILITIES AND ELDERLY CARERS

There are proportionately more elderly people amongst the general population and proportionately fewer younger people to help to look after them. These issues affect everybody – not just people with learning disabilities. People with severe or multiple disabilities live longer than was the case in the past. Therefore, a higher proportion of people attending day services for people with learning disabilities is likely to be older today than a decade ago. There are other forms of day services – many would say not enough – for other elderly people, including people with dementia. Some people with learning disabilities may appropriately move on to these services. For example, a person with Down's syndrome, expected to develop dementia as they become older, may be referred to services for people with dementia. This process is not without difficulties, as a case study in a companion book in the *Case Studies* series (Chapman and Marshall 1993) illustrates.

Chapter 7 considers the problems of older clients and their aging carers in detail, including cases where carers have died. Several of these studies illustrate the resilience of the extended family to come to the support of relatives. Often they themselves need support to do this.

Where day services have been moving in the direction of preparing people for change, becoming elderly as well as disabled will be easier to manage. For example, in such cases, people with learning disabilities will have already left their family homes and will be living with necessary support in ordinary housing. Others will be in group homes.

For many, this is still not the case. A point has been reached of 'no way out', of extreme mutual dependence in the relationships between carers and cared for. Each depends on the other – parents have as much a need to care for their adult children who have remained at home as the children have a need of their parents. Yet, as we have said, this situation cannot last. What can day services offer in this case?

Parents in this kind of situation seek a sense of security that their son or daughter will continue to be cared for. Community care as a whole can respond in terms of a guarantee of a home for life, backed by appropriate support. Day services will often be the key part of such support. At the same time, day services can help to prepare parents for the possibility of their sons of daughters living more independently.

The studies in Chapter 7 address these issues in detail. Other examples are Freddy in Chapter 4 and Tim in Chapter 9.

5. PEOPLE WITH MULTIPLE DISABILITIES

People with 'multiple disabilities' are not a homogeneous group and often different specialist forms of day service provision will be required to meet their varied needs. For example, some people will have, in addition to a learning disability, one or more of the following additional impairments or health problems:

- visual impairment
- hearing impairment
- epilepsy
- cerebral palsy
- consequences of brain damage
- a rare condition or syndrome
- a chest and/or heart complaint
- autism
- other illness or disability.

Several of the case studies illustrate the additional needs that people in one or more of these categories present. Peter, for example (Chapter 6), has severe epilepsy. Jeffrey and Jane (Chapter 5) have cerebral palsy, which, in the case of Richard (Chapter 6) means that he is quadriplegic.

Sometimes, aspects of these disabilities or health issues have been neglected in the case of people with learning disabilities. They are entitled to highly specialist assessment and sophisticated care and programme planning.

6. CHALLENGING BEHAVIOUR

People with learning disabilities are described as having 'challenging behaviour' when their behaviour makes demands on carers and on services which cannot easily be met. In rare cases, aggressive behaviour is associated with a specific medical condition. Drugs in such cases may reduce the incidence of such behaviour (as was possibly true in the case of Richard, discussed in Chapter 6). More often, 'challenging behaviour' is the outcome of frustration, poor communication of needs and, sometimes, sheer boredom (see Andy in Chapter 8).

People with profound and multiple disabilities, especially if they are large and heavy when it comes to assistance and management, are likely to present elements of challenging behaviour (see the example of Jane in Chapter 5). However, sometimes people who have a severe or profound learning disability and who are also physically fit and strong and able-bodied can also present challenging behaviour. This group has perhaps received insufficient attention. We therefore include an example in Chapter 9 – showing how boredom and frustration can be addressed through enhancing opportunities for risk-taking and learning.

7. CLIENTS WHO MAY BE INAPPROPRIATELY PLACED

Some people have been inappropriately referred to learning disability services perhaps because this was all that was available at the time. This is true, for example, in the case of some people suffering from the long-term consequences of severe head injuries. Alternative services are often not yet available, but should be developed as a result of a needs-led approach to service design in accordance with care in the community principles (Headway, National Head Injuries Association).

Others have drifted into day services for people with learning disabilities where other forms of support might have been more helpful and effective. An example is William discussed in Chapter 7.

8. EQUAL OPPORTUNITIES

'Equal opportunities' is a popular expression with many dimensions For example, it means equal opportunities with regard to:

- people from different racial and cultural backgrounds
- men and women
- people from materially well off and poorer social backgrounds
- people of different age-groups
- people with access to city amenities and people living in rural or remote areas
- married and single people, and so on.

Learning disabilities cut across these differences yet they are not always adequately reflected in the way day services are run or in terms of their accessibility. For example, fewer people from ethnic minorities attend day services than one would have expected – and fewer such people are to be found amongst day service staff.

'Equal' does not always mean 'the same'. Equality is about fairness in terms of access, opportunity, choice and support. People with physical disabilities want the facility to access a building using a ramp, where necessary, instead of steps. Able-bodied people may prefer to use steps. People from ethnic minorities may sometimes prefer to be approached about services through their own culturally acceptable leadership channels rather than through the expected formal welfare referral systems.

9. HOLISTIC PLANNING

Service design and programme planning are based on what we call 'needs-led' assessment. Services should be flexible enough to fit the needs of people, not the other way round. This is easier to proclaim than to achieve because traditionally buildings have been designed without sufficient reference to the needs of the people who will use them – or sometimes without knowing who these people will be and the sort of needs they will have. Classifications of need have not always had relevance to real people but have more to do with societal attitudes towards people whose needs have not been fully accepted or understood. Care in the community provides an opportunity to change attitudes – and its effective implementation depends on attitudes being changed.

It has to be recognised that 'needs' are not something to be attached to individuals in isolation but are to be understood in a social context. The needs of someone attending a day centre have to be understood in the social context of their home, parents' needs, brothers and sisters and other relations, friends, other sources of professional and informal help, and in terms of interests and opportunities and access to amenities in their localities.

'Holistic' also refers to every aspect of a person's humanity. It addresses the physical, mental, social and spiritual dimensions of living.

CHAPTER THREE

The Use of Social Networks

The cases studied in this volume have been assessed using a social network approach. This approach, developed over the past twenty years by the author and colleagues as a means of understanding the relationship between needs and services, is now incorporated in general textbooks in social work (Seed 1990) and for community care assessments (Seed and Kaye 1994). The value of using a social network approach more generally to understand people's needs and to plan services on this basis is widely acknowledged.

Social networks encapsulate some of the dimensions of an holistic approach summarised in the last chapter. A social network represents answers to the basic questions: 'Which people, places and activities are important in daily living? Why are they important? What does each part contribute to enhancing quality of life? What further support is needed to maximise the potentiality of the network?'

A service evaluation based on this approach incorporates information about the following:

- client's family and social background
- client's health problems and restrictions these problems impose
- client's sensory impairments and the restrictions these impose
- support needs with particular reference to self-care (e.g. dressing, feeding, washing), communication and daily living tasks
- client's interests and support needed to pursue them

- formal services, received from all sources
- service reviews
- progress or regress regarding learning and support needs
- informal services and help received from all sources, including family, neighbours, volunteers etc
- holiday experiences
- a picture of daily life
- an enquiry into features or 'qualities' of key relationships
- client's views, choices and preferences
- carers' perspectives – including their own limitations and health issues.

All of this information, put together, provides the background for asking:

- What activities are being pursued at day services?
- Do these activities reflect a programme of aims and expectations?
- What are the objectives and the expectations for each activity within each programme?

A day service is understood and evaluated in terms of asking: 'Does it enrich daily living?'

The case studies begin with a summary of personal and social background and with reference to any health issues. Statements are then made about support needs. Then details are given about the daily life of the person at home and at the centre. This information is based on diaries kept by clients, with a degree of assistance required to do this in individual circumstances, for monitored fortnights. An example will be found in Figure 7.3 (Page 79). Information collected from the diaries is then analysed and represented in diagrammatic form using the standard symbols shown in Figure 3.1.

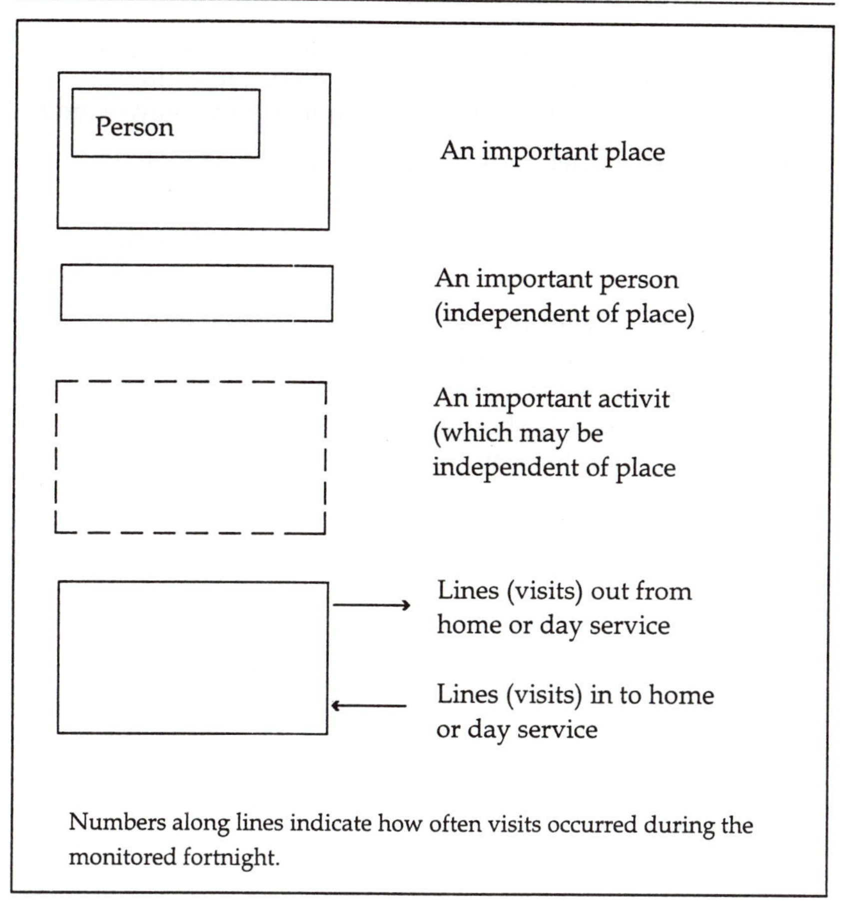

Figure 3.1 Key to network diagrams

These network diagrams provide a representation at a glance of what life is like for someone attending a day service (or any other service). They have to be interpreted in the context of the other material, including social background, the person's views and choices, their carers' perspective and 'relationship qualities'. These qualities include the extent to which a key relationship is:

- instrumental in delivering practical help or advice
- a gateway to contacts and help from others

- a medium for friendship or other sentient features which are important to the person concerned (i.e. it could be someone to *dislike* although this is not often acknowledged!)
- a source of influence (which might be beneficial or detrimental)
- a source of recognition as to the intrinsic worth of the person
- an opportunity for the person with a learning disability to reciprocate any of the above relationship features or qualities – i.e. a chance for them to offer practical help or advice to others, to show affection, to be a gateway to contacts with others, and so on.

CHAPTER FOUR

Promoting Quality of Life at Home

A number of issues are raised in this chapter about the fit between the centre and the home situation. The home situation incorporates the client and other members of the family. We assess needs at home by looking at the family lifestyle and the client's home-based social network.

Home situations vary in terms of the following:

- Who is at home to care? In particular, what is the situation of the main support person?
- What are the dependency needs of other members of the family?
- What are the attitudes and 'orientation' of family members, i.e. to what extent are they oriented to 'the world of learning disability' or to pursuing a 'normal' family life?
- To what extent is the family supported by relatives?
- What other sources of support does the family have?
- Does the family have easy access to community facilities?
- Are the parents' attitudes to the person with the handicap 'supportive' or 'protective' in respect of risk-taking, making independent choices, making friends, learning to live more independently?

Further questions relate to past schooling. Where this experience was poor, the question arises: Can day services compensate?

These issues are discussed with reference to two cases, Freddy and Charles. Both of them have Down's syndrome. Both had severe learning disabilities and fairly similar support needs. Both also came from single parent families. In other respects, however, their home situations varied. For example, Freddy lived with his mother whereas Charles lived with his father.

FREDDY

1984

Freddy, aged 28, lived with his elderly mother alone in a council flat in an inner city urban area. Five other brothers and sisters had left home. As will be seen from the network for the first monitored fortnight (Figure 4.1 and 4.2) these, and other relations, together with neighbours played a part in Freddy's life at home. The family did not have a car and Freddy travelled with his mother by taxi on some occasions – for shopping or to visit relations – but on most occasions they walked.

People with Down's syndrome vary enormously in their support needs. Freddy had greater support needs than many others at this particular centre. He needed assistance with practically all aspects of self-management and daily living tasks – with the exception that he was a good walker. Indeed the mother said he would never stop walking unless told to. 'He has no idea of turning round and coming back,' she said. He had to be accompanied always. He had difficulty when he came to stairs and needed assistance, even when there was a handrail.

Freddy, however, was quite crafty in some situations. He could, for example, unlock the windows by taking his mother's walking-stick and hooking it round the lock. His vocabulary was reasonable although strangers would have difficulty in understanding him. He could only communicate choices and basic needs with people he knew really well. He had some fears – for example he was frightened of swimming pools, bridges over rushing water and the wind at night. He slept at home in the same room as his mother.

The mother acknowledged that, 'Having been in nursing, you tend to be really safety conscious'. She explained she never let him use boiling water or sharp knives: 'I don't let him butter bread though I dare say he knows how to do it.' Money did not mean anything to Freddy – he had no interest in it. On the other hand he could do things like setting the table at home. His mother explained he might not get a knife and fork the right way round but he knew where to put them and what to bring out for each meal, e.g. cutlery

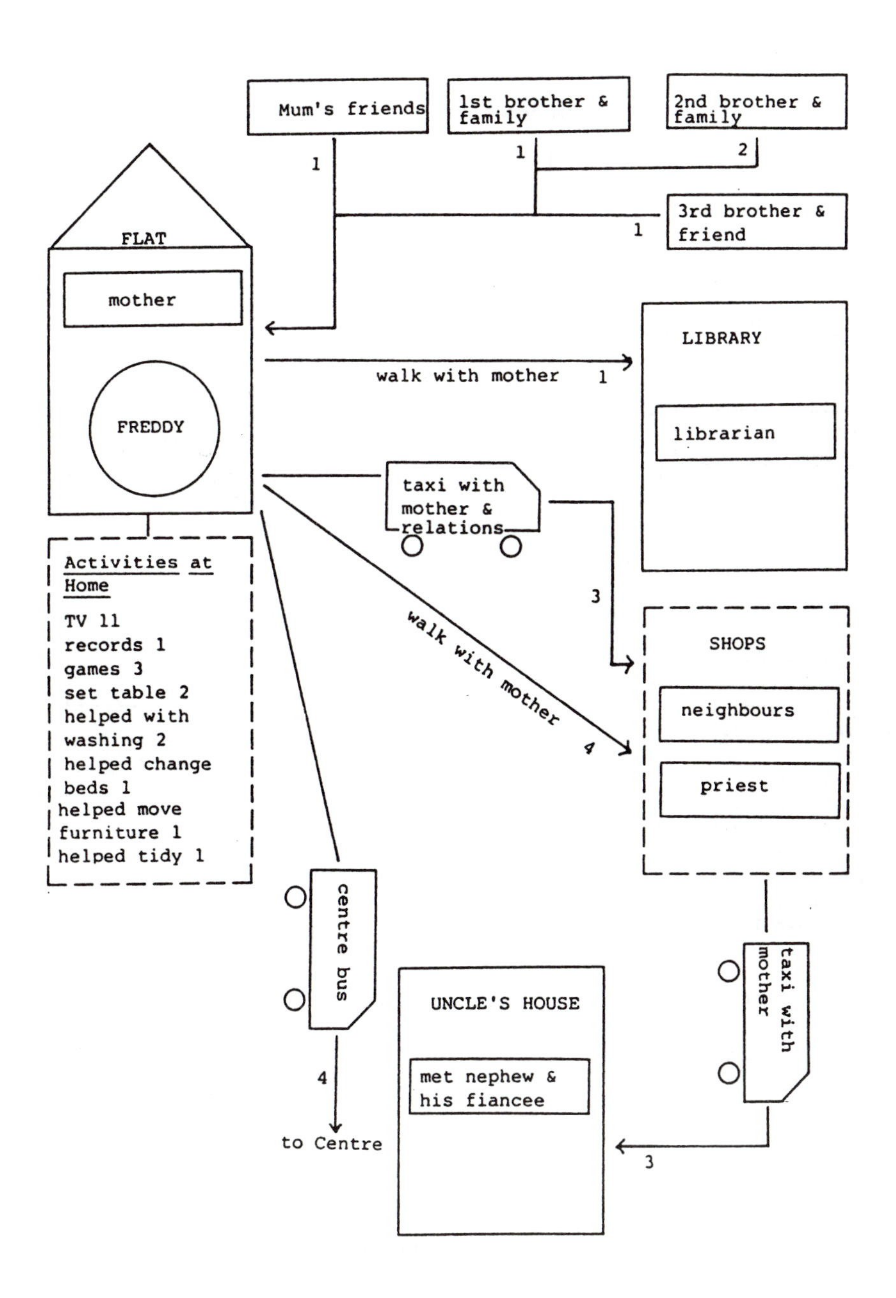

Figure 4.1 Freddy – first monitored fortnight at the home (1984)

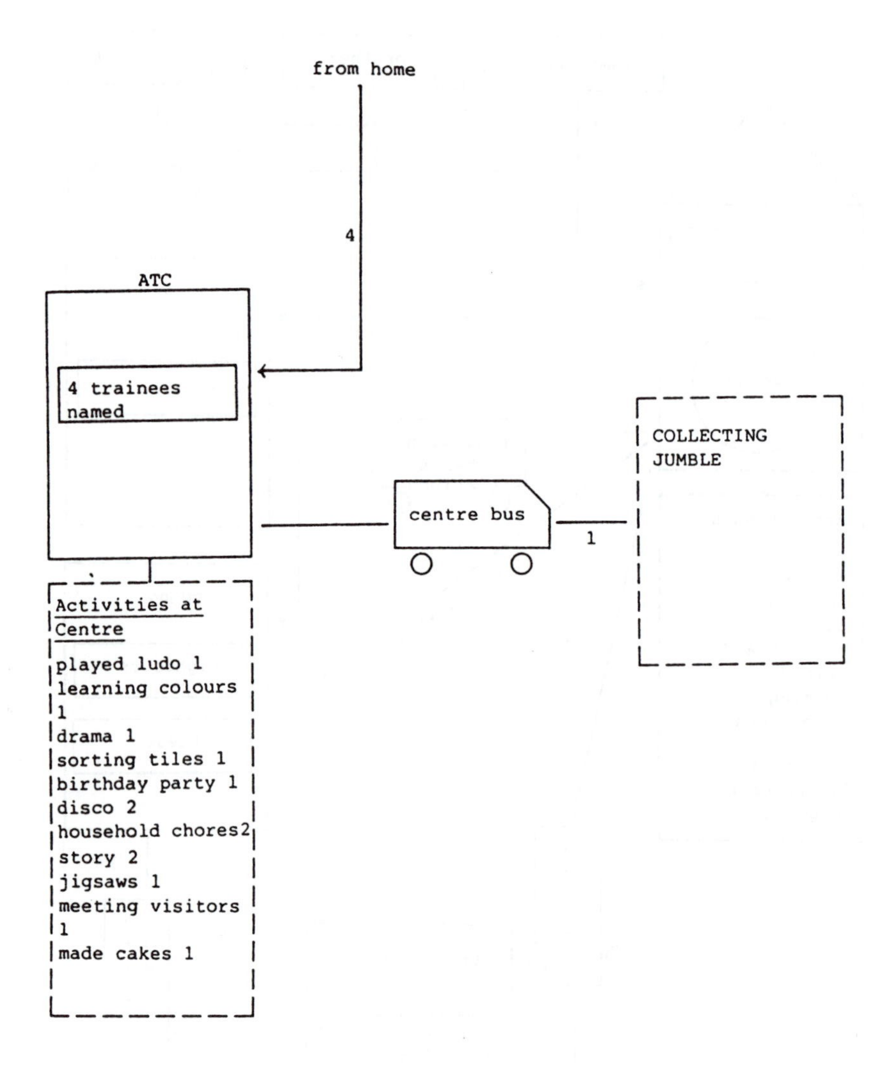

Figure 4.2 Freddy – first monitored fortnight at the centre (1984)

and sauces. His mother commented: 'Sometimes it's surprising what he can do. For example, he can use the record player and last week he learnt very quickly how to use the remote control on our new television including how to get the four different channels.' His mother described him as a caring person and this extended to objects as well as people. In particular he did not like bursting balloons. 'It's as though he feels the balloon is active and that its life is ending. That probably sounds daft but that's how I think he feels and he manages to convey this.'

The researcher evaluating the day service in 1984 reflected:

> The importance of the centre to both mum and Freddy is rooted in the history of Freddy starting to attend. After leaving school, mum had tried to get a place at the centre for Freddy but none had been available. That was 13 years ago, and until two years ago, Freddy had stayed at home with mum and dad. The effect of this had been that when Freddy did eventually come to the notice of the social service department again, mum was reluctant to accept the place at the day centre, preferring Freddy to stay at home with her. It had taken several visits from the centre staff working with Freddy in the home, before she felt able to allow Freddy to attend the centre. Mum is now grateful for both the place, and the gradual approach taken by the staff in introducing both herself and Freddy to the idea of his being away from his mum for two days a week. Earlier on in Freddy's life, the mother said she had had to fight to get her son a place in a school and he did not attend until secondary schooling started. He then attended a special unit but the mother said he was not happy there.

The centre Freddy attended was in some ways very unlike most other day services at that time. Attendance was part-time and confined to certain days of the week (see Chapter 8 for a fuller description of this centre). Freddy's key worker at the centre described the centre aim as being 'to give people more scope, a better lifestyle, an improved quality of life'. Obviously, he said, the ultimate aim is independent living but for some people this is not going to be possible. So far as Freddy was concerned his key worker thought he was going to have to go into residential care fairly soon. The centre had been able to introduce him gradually to a larger number of people, thus lessening the impact on his having to go into residential care when his mother would become too old to cope. This would make the transition a lot easier.

Freddy attended the centre on two days a week, Tuesdays and Thursdays. The Tuesday activities, together with some of the staff objectives and comments were as follows for the first monitored fortnight:

Activity	*Objectives and Comments*
Household chores	Good movement and understanding of simple chores. Freddy is capable of doing the chores. He did well and showed Henry (another trainee) how to squeeze clothes
Read and discussed fairy story *Hansel and Gretel*	Enjoyment of *Grimm's Fairy Tales* – lots of pictures. 'He was less interested in the fairy tale than Ethel (trainee helper) and myself (staff)'
Games activities – Freddy did jigsaw in company with other trainees. Followed by video party	Freddy needs to be with the other trainees during the afternoon. He must learn to rub along with them. They must tolerate his continuous noises. The video was preparation Christmas celebrations (late November). Freddy half-heartedly did the jigsaw – he sat with another trainee who torments him. She sat down beside him. He ate crisps but did not offer any to her. During the party he was part of the group
(The following week):	
Magic painting and trying to learn colours	Use of paintbrush and water – to keep work clean. We covered red and green recognition. Freddy did well this morning once we got him started. He is still making funny noises even when requested to stop

Reading and looking at pictures of *Hansel and Gretel*	Sitting without making funny noises and showing interest in story-book
Pantomime – *Hansel and Gretel*	Trainees participate playing the parts in turn
Part of the group – making the witch's house and cages.	Freddy enjoyed the pantomime. He is getting a bit cheeky with me – Great! When told about it he smiles charmingly
Follow-up of morning story	Learning to hiss and boo rather than 'konking'

Staff comment for the day as a whole read:

> All the trainees accept Freddy – sometimes they try to help him quieten but they are never unkind to him. He is very friendly with Andrew (another less able trainee) and the two of them have competitions to see who can make the funniest noise.

Activities and objectives for Thursday were as follows:

Activity	*Objectives and Comments*
Made chocolate crispy cakes to take home and for afternoon tea. Washed up dishes	He washed his hands. He put cake cases into cake tins. Under supervision he melted the up dishes chocolate and made crispy cakes. Occasionally licked his fingers. Hoovered up spilt crispies. He was excellent but 'pulled the plug of the hoover out of the wall switch after I asked him not to do so'. Otherwise he was very co-operative

Lunch: met visitors – 'How do you do?'	Was polite to visitors
Played ludo instead of watching the video film *Sound of Music* which he refused to do	He shook dice, took his turn and watching video film enjoyed the game. Put the board away. He made a candle with another trainee. He likes to choose what to do!

The comment for the day by the staff person read:

> There was a nice incident at lunchtime. For some reason Freddy was not given a pudding. He told some of the trainees who did not understand.
>
> When the extra puddings were carried up to our living room Freddy went up there, lifted a pudding, brought it down to the dining room and ate it.

Freddy was sick during the following Thursday but, in other weeks, activities would follow a similar kind of structure for each separate day. Trainees were able at this centre to attend a third day on a drop-in basis but this was entirely voluntary and Freddy did not do so.

At this time the mother saw the purposes of Freddy's attendance as being to give him something useful to do and to give her time to herself. She also recognised the centre's social function and commented that he was much more outgoing. 'He's changed – he's better in everything, more communicative.' She was very happy with the centre and with the staff.

Diaries kept by Freddy's mother give us a picture of life at home at this time. Here are some of the entries for two of the days.

> **Sunday 25 November:**
>
> Freddy up at 10.30 am and has his weekend breakfast of sausage, bacon, eggs and potato scones. As all the family and I have decided to paint my front door, we went to a big do-it-yourself store to get the paint etc.

Freddy was happy helping and pushing the trolley. We all had dinner and wrote out our overseas Christmas cards and stamped them. At about eight everyone went home and Freddy was a bit sad but soon perked up.

Wednesday 28 November:

Freddy was quite weepy when he got up, didn't eat his breakfast so I didn't fuss him and tried to get him back to his usual self. We went to the shops but Freddy wasn't interested. At the shop he never even chose a cake or anything to take up with us on our weekly visit. After tea we went up to my brother's for our weekly visit and Freddy brightened up and their wee dog made a real fuss of him. I eventually discovered the cause of Freddy's upset. It was because he thought his brother (who had arrived from Dublin) would be staying with us for a few days, as he always had a great rapport with Jack, but he will stay overnight before going back to Dublin. We will go to the airport with him as he is leaving his car with one of my nephews. I am hoping Freddy will understand that Jack has gone, for a while anyhow.

1986

Some 16 months after this, there was a second monitored fortnight. The activities and events in Freddy's life are depicted in Figures 4.3 and 4.4. If anything, life was now more hectic and involved with relations than during the first fortnight. During this same period Freddy still attended the centre on Tuesdays and Thursdays only. The following are the activities and objectives given by staff for Freddy during this fortnight:

Activity	*Objectives and Comments*
Hand work – games hour+ e.g. for five minutes	To encourage him to concentrate, Freddy was loathe to do much – so we just wanted to keep him involved. We wanted to find out what he was able to do and build on it

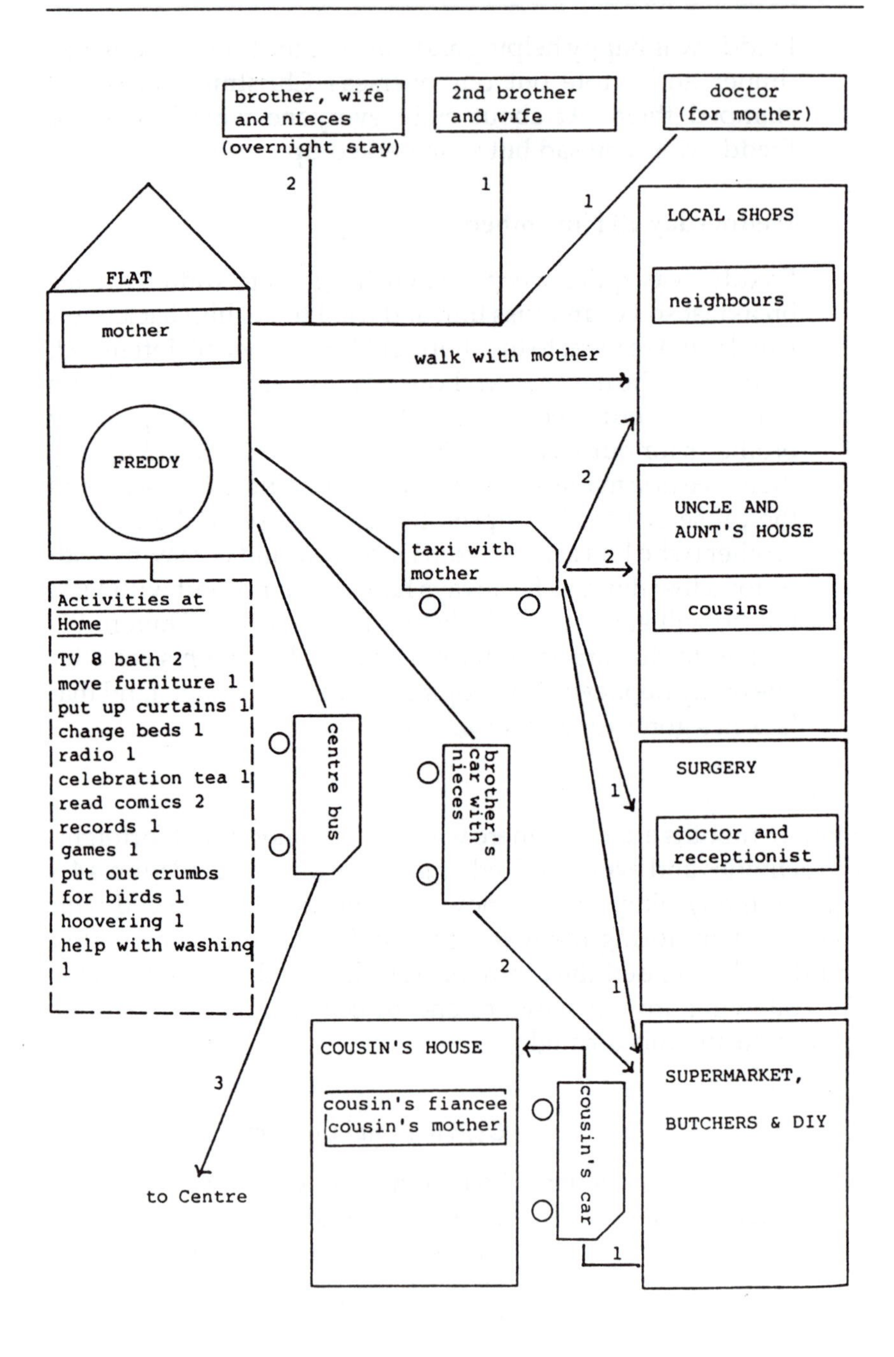

Figure 4.3 Freddy – second monitored fortnight at home (1986)

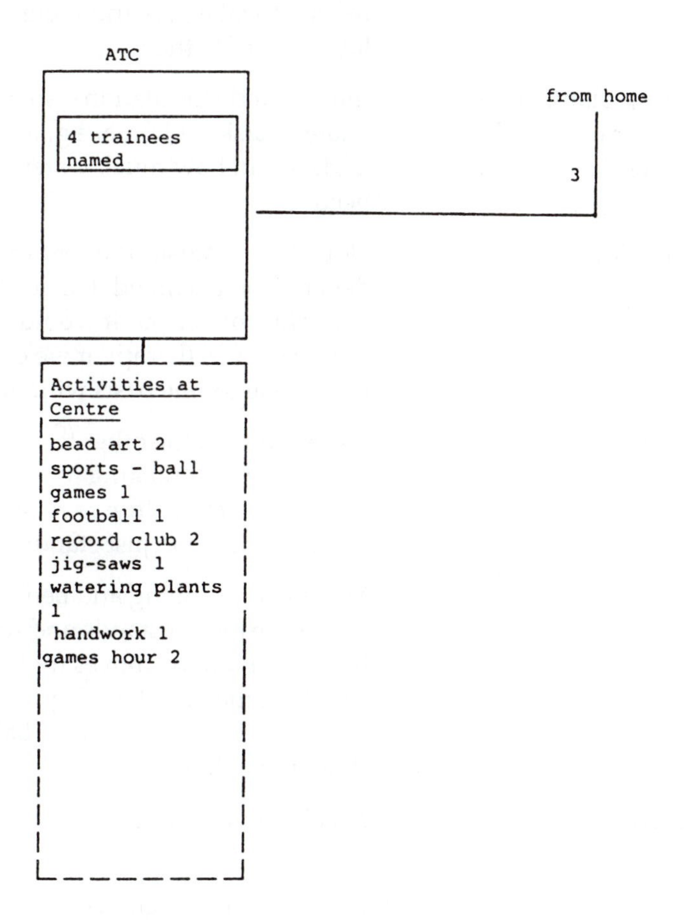

Figure 4.4. Freddy – second monitored fortnight at the centre (1986)

Jigsaws	This arose because he refused to go to a bowling match. The object was to encourage him to join in some sort of activity – socially. Sometimes he refuses to take part and there's not a lot you can do then
Watering plants with another trainee in the countryside	Interest and stimulation – so he can relate to tasks at home, e.g. to understand how much water etc. you need
Record club	Hope to use music as a therapy. It depends on his mood. He doesn't really like music but it would perhaps act as therapy if we could do it on a one-to-one basis with him
Sports sessions	To join in with the other trainees rather than just relating to staff.Trying to get him to relate to others rather than just standing back.
	Movement, running and bending – otherwise he just stands and rocks. Important that he moves for his health. Some days he will join in but mostly he wants to pass the ball to staff all the time
Bead art+	No objectives stated

Key:
* Major activity, i.e. at least two full days or equivalent during monitored period
** Main activity, i.e. at least half the time during the monitored period
+ Activity described as 'very important' by staff
++ Activity described as 'crucially important' by staff

The staff were still concerned to help Freddy mix and communicate. The relationship of this to home was that he should be weaned away from the very close involvement with his family so that in the long run he could live more independently. So what happened, we may ask, on the days during the week when Freddy was not attending the centre? The following are some examples taken from the home diary during the second monitored fortnight:

> **Monday 10 March:**
>
> Freddy slept until dinner-time then didn't want to eat very much. In the afternoon he watched television and listened to his radio. He had tea and ate a little but had plenty of fluids. Watched television and had his bath to get ready for tomorrow at the centre. Freddy has had a heavy cold and cough and was indoors all weekend and today.
>
> **Wednesday 12 March:**
>
> The doctor visited and as I (mother) had a very painful bout of arthritis in my fingers I was having pain killers and an injection. As Freddy vanished to his bedroom whilst the doctor was in, I had the doctor arrange a visit to the hospital for a blood test for him as I think he has too little thyroid in his system, as he just wants to sit about or sleep. In the evening we went out to my sister-in-law's for our usual weekly visit and Freddy just sat about not his usual self.
>
> **Friday 14 March:**
>
> Appointment at doctor's surgery for Freddy and I. He had blood taken and sent to hospital for a thyroid diagnosis. Results in a fortnight or so. In the afternoon went with Freddy to supermarket and when we arrived at checkout he had added a selection of his own.
>
> Had tea and Freddy read his comics and watched television then listened to country and western records.

At the weekends life became hectic with visiting relatives.

Saturday 15 March:

Freddy slept late as he usually does on Saturdays. My son and wife and granddaughter arrived for their usual weekend visit. We all went to the supermarket to do the weekend and weekly shopping. My other two grandchildren arrived also. After tea we had everyone deciding what to watch on television, with Freddy winning. Freddy just loves a full house and hates it when everyone goes.

After the second monitored fortnight we asked the mother to give us further details of the most significant people and places for Freddy. The most significant places were all the homes of various relatives. For example, at his cousin's house, 'he enjoys playing darts there and listening to records'. At his sister's house, he 'enjoys the company and their dog who is very good with him'. Not surprisingly, all the significant people were also relations. An aunt was helpful in increasing access to other people, including friends of relations as well as other relatives. It was interesting that she was not regarded as being of any relevance in practical terms, i.e. in terms of what we call 'instrumental qualities'. Affection featured prominently and also Freddy was enabled to do practical things to help the aunt.

This aunt had agreed to take Freddy in the event of anything happening to his mother. Another relative was important because he had a car and could take Freddy and his mother out. The third relative was important and because, amongst other things, 'she plays football and will play it with Freddy whenever she visits'.

The mother felt there was a very close relationship between herself and the centre staff. Parent workshops are held and the mother said these were 'definitely to be recommended. I've always enjoyed them.' She also welcomed the diary. The mother described this as a record 'for all time so that if anything should happen to me they can be referred to, to see how he's been over the years'. Especially earlier on, staff used to come up to visit Freddy at home and she appreciated this.

In summary, it seemed that a pattern of life was being sustained for Freddy in which he was happy in the company of those he knew, especially his family and those he knew at the centre. He is moody and his physical health was not always good. There was close contact between the mother and the centre and specific problems could be dealt with as they arose. But the centre key worker had a more long-term goal, thinking ahead to the future when Freddy might be able, or have to, leave home.

At the end of the second monitored period the researcher asked about progress that had been made since the first period. At the centre they thought that there had been definite progress in communication and specific words that had been learnt were mentioned. At home the mother agreed. She said he continued to improve with his speech. She added, 'I think it's being amongst the others at the centre.' During the home visit when this information was obtained the researcher noted that Freddy knew immediately how a new heater worked although the researcher hadn't worked it out herself. He does seem to have a forte for mechanical things. There was no evidence that this was being exploited either at home or at the centre.

In reflecting on this case at the end of the research period it was noted:

> Although Freddy's diaries show a reasonably active fortnight, the activities are all done with mum, and involve visits to relatives or visits from relatives. The activities at the centre are perhaps more 'play activities' than might be appropriate for his needs. However I think they are no more so than they would be at other centres. There are definite learning expectations in these activities, for example learning to take his turn, learning to tolerate and be tolerated by other people in the room. I cannot help questioning, however, whether it might be more useful for Freddy to learn how to put a kettle on than to make chocolate crispies... I do think we need to explore whether some of the activities done in day centres achieve the almost slogan-like aims that staff give. Does sorting tiles lead to trainees being able to differentiate between different colours and shapes, or is this learning not transferred to other tasks? Can in fact this learning take place when a trainee is left to get on with the task himself, receiving only perhaps one-ninth of the instructor's attention? Are there no tasks that can be developed which would practise a similar skill, but with perhaps more 'real life' meaning?

1988

In gaining permission from the mother to use this material she told me that she was still concerned over Freddy's future residential needs in the event of her no longer being able to look after him. She was now aged 72. She felt she could not expect other family members to look after him: 'They have their own lives.' Meantime she said her own arthritis had been better.

The mother also mentioned a number of other features at the day centre. There is bingo for parents every fortnight and a parents' committee has been established. She also welcomed the fact that welfare rights officer is due to visit the centre.

Freddy himself had recently had to go to hospital to have his teeth extracted. The mother stayed two nights in the hospital with him and helped to nurse him.

1995

Freddy's mother is now very elderly and her health has, indeed, deteriorated. She has had to leave home and a relative has moved in to support Freddy. Freddy has become depressed and aggressive and, a few months ago, he refused to continue to attend the day centre. A project worker outside the centre is trying to encourage him to accept a residential place but he is resisting this. Respite is being attempted as a step towards a permanent residential place.

POINTS FOR DISCUSSION

1. Despite Freddy's Down's condition being obvious from an early age the kind of services that one might have expected were not available. How do you suppose the family coped at all in this case without such services?
2. In what ways would you say Freddy was disadvantaged on account of not having education appropriate to his special needs at an early age and the possibility of going to a day centre on leaving school? Can the centre compensate for this?
3. What part do relatives play in Freddy's pattern of living?
4. Compare the quality of life for Freddy a) on days he attends the centre, b) on weekdays when he does not attend the centre and c) at weekends

5. What difference does it make in this case that the family does not have a car?
6. Can you suggest possible explanations for (a) the mother's reluctance to let Freddy go out to a day centre at first and (b) Freddy's own reluctance to go out often except with people he knows well?
7. What difference does it make a) to Freddy and b) to his mother that attendance at this particular centre is part-time? Would you say part-time attendance was particularly appropriate in this case?
8. Does part-time attendance meet the mother's need for respite during the daytime?
9. Consider in detail the activities and objectives of staff during each of the monitored fortnights. Do you agree with the researcher's reflections at the end regarding some of these activities?
10. What are the benefits of close contacts between the mother and the centre in this case? Discuss the forms of contact. What forms of contact do you think are generally most advantageous and why, e.g. parents' meetings, diaries, visits to the centre, home visits by centre staff etc.?
11. Consider the mother's comment that it is not fair to ask relations to look after Freddy and that he should continue to be prepared for living in a residential setting?
12. Do you agree with the centre's aim of preparing Freddy for a place in a hostel? (Note that the mother was not in good health and that another relation had offered to take Freddy if anything should happen to his mother.)
13. Consider the changes that have taken place in the family situation over the past ten years or so. Are you surprised that Freddy has become depressed and aggressive? With hindsight, could more have been done to help Freddy leave his mother's care earlier? How? (Bear in mind the importance of client choice and that Freddy was content to stay with his mother.)

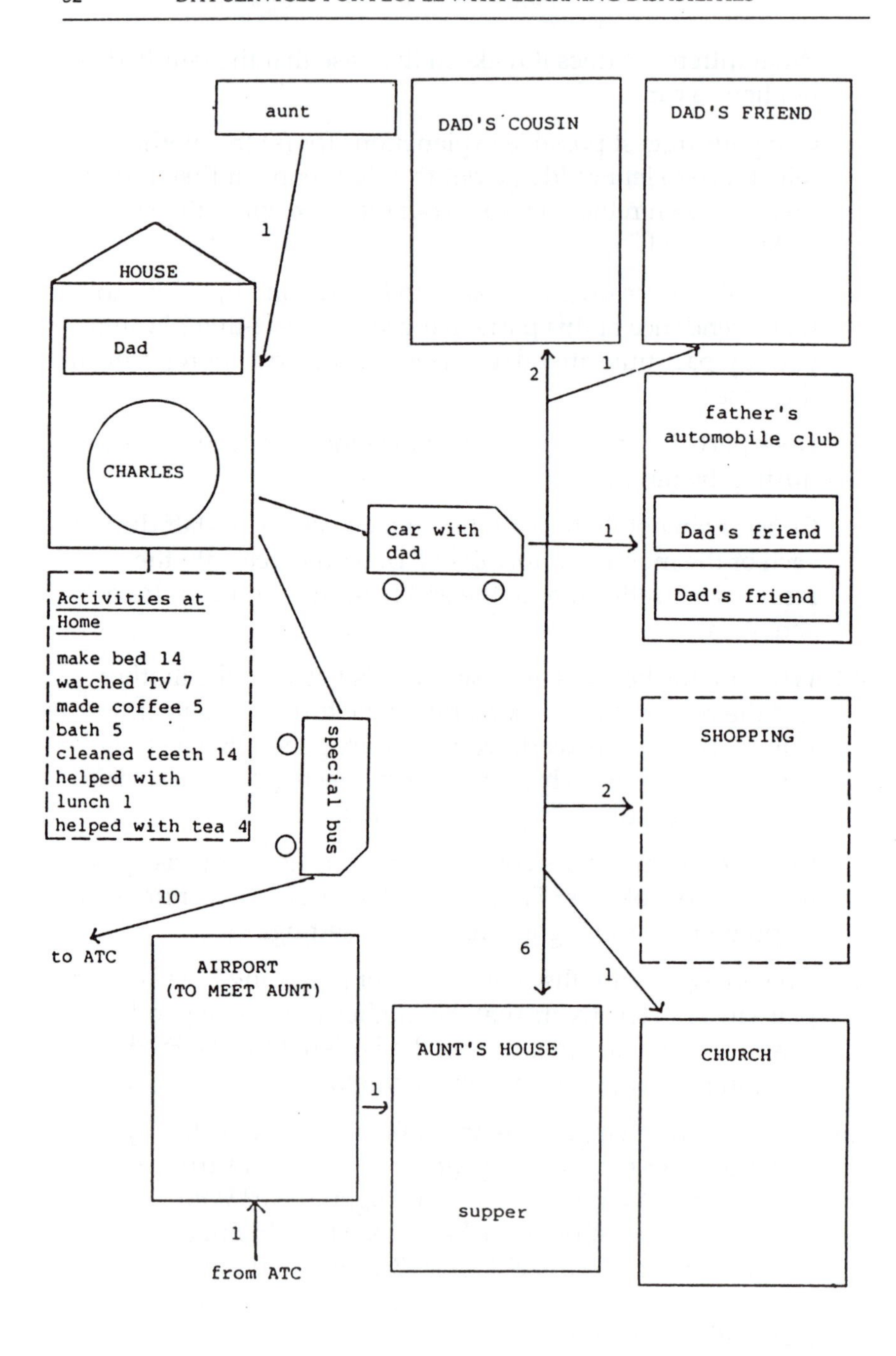

Figure 4.5 Charles – first monitored fortnight at home (1985)

CHARLES

1985

Charles was aged 27 and he lived at home with his father. His mother had died about 18 months before the study started. His father was retired and was able to spend a good deal of time with Charles. In considering the network for the first monitored fortnight (see Figure 4.5) the researcher commented that 'Charles could be pretty isolated without his father's contacts as he goes everywhere with his dad.' However, 'life is reasonably varied, consisting of visits to his aunt's house, where father and he regularly have their tea, visits to his father's friends and on one occasion going to his father's automobile club with him. Church also appears on the network.'

The family lived in a private semi-detached house in a quiet estate within a city. The centre Charles attended was 15 minutes' walk away, or on a bus route.

Charles, like Freddy, has Down's syndrome. That fact does not tell us, in itself, anything about the extent of his support needs with regard to self-management and daily living. Below are some of the comments recorded from the father's perspective and from the perspective of staff at the centre.

Support Needs

Activity	*At Home*	*At the Centre*
Dressing	No problems (during the monitoring it transpired that father or sometimes aunt, tied his laces)	Problems tying laces
Washing and toilet	No problems	Not sure about showers. He is meticulous about washing himself
Eating and drinking	No problems	No problems

Activity	*At Home*	*At the Centre*
Mobility, including climbing stairs	A wee bit slow. Aunt will encourage him, e.g. by going 'left, right'	No problems
Preparation of food	He can make coffee. He could make himself a sandwich	Only if assisted
Household tasks	He makes his bed each day. This has been his duty for some years now. He can hoover with a carpet sweeper. He likes watering the plants	He washes dishes and tidies up
Understanding of money	He recognises the 10p coin but I don't think he understands any others	He knows about some coins but not their value
Getting out and about outside the house or outside the centre	There is always someone with him either in or out of the house	No problems
Making himself understood to strangers	No problems	Only with a great deal of difficulty
Other comments		He sticks to routine. He needs to do this or he gets quite confused. He is quite witty at times

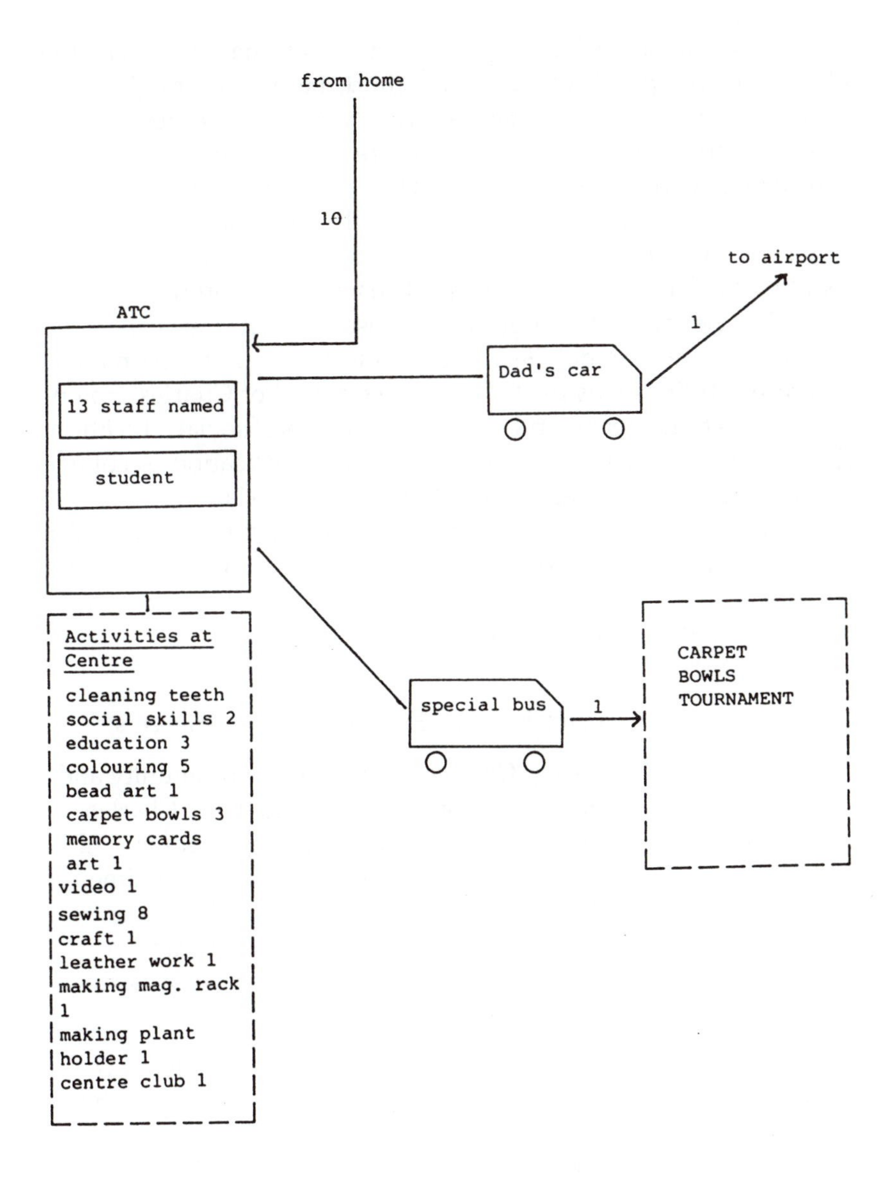

Figure 4.6 Charles – first monitored fortnight at the centre (1985)

The centre also noted other comments about his behaviour but we will return to these later.

Charles had attended a special school. He had also had the advantages of speech therapy as a child. He went straight from school to an 'occupation centre' shortly before the centre was redesignated as an 'adult training centre'. Four years later he was transferred to his present centre. This was described to the researcher as catering for all but 'profoundly handicapped'.

Because of limitations to the building it could also not cope with people who, on account of physical disabilities, could not climb steps. The centre was thought to be closest to what we called the further education model (Seed 1988). This means that a main focus in centre activities was the fullest development of Charles' potential in educational terms and especially in terms of social education. The centre had links with a college of further education. A college lecturer saw all clients at the centre on a daily basis.

Figure 4.6 shows Charles' activities and network at the centre during the first monitored fortnight fairly soon after the beginning of the research. Some of the staff expectations and comments for these activities are listed below:

Activity	*Staff Objectives, Expectations and Comments*
Social skills education	To help Charles cope with the community and make him more acceptable to them. Charles has problems reading social signs but is well cared for and behaves well most of the time. He can be very babyish at times. He never quarrels with other trainees but he can be moody if teased – although he is very easily got out of his moods
Personal hygiene program	Shave, clean and polish own shoes. He was expected to shave himself, clean and polish his own shoes, put on his shoes and tie laces. He managed unsupervised and nobody helped to tie his laces. His behaviour was very good
Recreation in quiet room (lunchtime)	To relax and socialise. Charles wanted to work on a piece of craft. He preferred to be on his own

Colouring and painting	To obtain paints and water brush; to mix colours into as many variations as possible. He did get water and brush but could not get paints as they were stuck in the containers. He did try a little to mix and then 'did his own thing'. He was rather lazy. He worked for 5 minutes and then rested for 15 minutes
Sewing	He will do the most simple tasks. He would be very neat at them and is usually very industrious. At present he will do all the simple tasks. He could do other more complicated work but he does not like changes. He was very well behaved and very quiet. When in a good mood he can be very witty. On the other hand he can be easily upset. Very introverted

These comments were obtained through staff diaries. At the end of each day the key staff person was invited to make a general comment and one such comment in Charles' case was the following: 'Nothing in particular happened today. As Charles is so introverted and shy he finds it difficult to volunteer information. Even during our little talk today Charles was close to tears.'

In contrast to being 'close to tears', however, Charles appeared to enjoy a particular event that week. This was taking part in a carpet bowling competition. The staff person commented that he 'had a great time at the competition. He was very pleased with himself as he won a medal.' The tournament was in competition with other centres and was held in the hall of an assessment centre. The staff commented, 'The hall was very cold. Everybody had to keep moving to keep warm. Our centre came in third in the team event.'

How far was all this relevant to Charles' needs at home? In answering this question, we will first consider what the staff saw as the relevance; second, what Charles himself felt and third, what his father thought.

Charles' key staff person said the aim of the centre in general was to make trainees more acceptable to the community, i.e. in behavioural terms. But for Charles, he concluded, what he likes doing is colouring. You're just really keeping him happy and occupied. You could help him learn how to dress and look after himself but you don't really have a chance to do this in a group'. He further commented that it was hard to get preparation time. He added, 'Sometimes I think they try too hard at the centre. We haven't time to do all the things we're trying to do.' He said that care assistants occasionally take two people out of a big group and show them how to do things – in Charles' case, for example, how to tie laces. However, in general it was clear to us that there was conflict between maintaining a centre routine for group activities, which was inevitable in terms of the limited numbers of staff available, and giving the individualised personal attention that people like Charles needed if they were ready to 'learn'. In other words the idea that a centre has educational objectives has to be sustained in individualised practice if it is to have meaning.

Another theme in some of the staff comments was the need to encourage Charles to do things for himself. In this case, the fact that activities are in groups and that not enough individual attention is available from staff may help. It is not possible, for example, to go around tying everybody's shoelaces and it is not possible to treat Charles different from the others. Thus in one instance we see that it was recorded that he did, in fact, manage to tie his own laces in this kind of situation. In other words, it appeared he did not need teaching but rather the little push to do it for himself confidently along with others. In a group, there could have been a competitive element which helped. On the other hand, we have to address ourselves to Charles' changing moods and the fact that sometimes at least he is unhappy at the centre. Too much of a purely educational slant in terms of 'acceptable behaviour' may mask other issues about his feelings and social relationships which are surely relevant to a social work service. Nowhere, in any of the staff diaries during the first monitored period is there any mention of the death of Charles' mother, just over 18 months previously, and of the possible effects this might have directly on his moods and in terms of the kind of life he lived at home.

In talking to Charles about why he came to the centre he simply said, 'I like it.' His favourite thing was sewing. He also liked attending a centre club which was held once a week in the evenings. However, the researcher commented that it was difficult for him to deal with these kinds of questions. He was very willing to help the researcher but it was difficult to 'make him understand'. He tended to say 'Yes' whichever way round the question was put so that sometimes he contradicted himself.

Incidentally, the researcher also observed how difficult it was for Charles to climb the centre stairs. Today I watched him holding the rail and when we met the manager on the stairs she praised him for using the rail. She said that Charles had particularly enjoyed a panel discussion they had had on health and safety and holding the rails was one of the topics covered.

Charles' father confirmed that he was very happy at the centre. He would not like to miss it. He enjoyed the company, and he liked going. The father thought that the company was the most important aspect of centre aims but it was also to get help in the activities he undertook. From the father's point of view, the centre also had a respite function on the weekly club night. He made a point of going out on that night by himself and it made a break from the usual pattern of activities undertaken jointly by father and son. It is perhaps interesting that the respite function of the centre is perceived by the father as consisting in an additional night-time activity and not in the routine day-time attendance. Because he is retired, he is able and happy to be with Charles during the day.

The father explained the importance of his sister, i.e. Charles' aunt in the home situation. The aunt had been away for part of the first monitoring fortnight (see Figure 4.6). Charles and his father met her at the airport and subsequently they went to the aunt's house for supper six times. The aunt also visited and was able to offer practical assistance, for example, in helping Charles with any dressing problems. The researcher noted the crucial importance to this family of the father's car. Without it, the social network would have been much more restricted.

The three most important people for Charles at home (apart from his father) appeared to be, according to his father, the aunt, a couple at the father's automobile social club and the father's cousin. We will look at each of these relationships separately.

The aunt was said to 'relate well and give practical assistance'. She was also a means of contact with other relations. 'Sometimes the cousin visits the aunt's while we're there.' The aunt helped in practical ways (what we call 'instrumental qualities') in terms of washing his hair, encouraging him in climbing stairs and involving him in cleaning his house – i.e. the aunt sometimes cleaned the house for the father. It was also a relationship of affection. 'He gets on well with her,' said the father. We asked whether there were ways in which the relationship enabled Charles to do things for the aunt in return and we were told that, yes, he would, for example, set the table for her.

In general, then, this was a warm supporting relationship. Was it too protective? Ultimately this is a matter of personal judgement in the light of what would be regarded as socially and culturally normal. Is it normal for a man of 27 years old to have his hair washed for him? Could he do this for himself? If so, was the centre able to make a contribution first, in terms of demonstrating to Charles at the centre that he could do it by himself and, second, in making an explicit link with the fact that this was done for him at home? However, we have to take into account social needs as well as purely behavioural patterns. Washing someone's hair is a very personal and affectionate thing to perform.

The second important relationship was with family friends described as 'a couple at the club'. The father explained, 'We visit them at home quite often and we may meet their relatives.' There was no particular practical help they gave to Charles but they were very kind to him. 'They really like him.' This last comment came in answer to our question about what we call 'reciprocal qualities'. In other words, Charles was able to give something to others because he was a likeable person and in turn he was liked for this.

The third significant person was the father's cousin. Again, as with the aunt, she helped him to talk and this too was a relationship of affection.

At the end of the study the researcher made her own assessment of the extent to which the attitude of the parent could be considered supportive or protective, in terms of what we call 'the prevailing attitude' towards particular aspects of living, and in general. The researcher concluded that the father was in general supportive and especially so in helping Charles to make new friends and in engaging in a wider range of activities. In other respects, however, there was no evidence. Because of the family car, in many ways such an advantage, Charles had no experience of using public transport at home. His opportunities for domestic self-management were limited (see Figure 4.6).

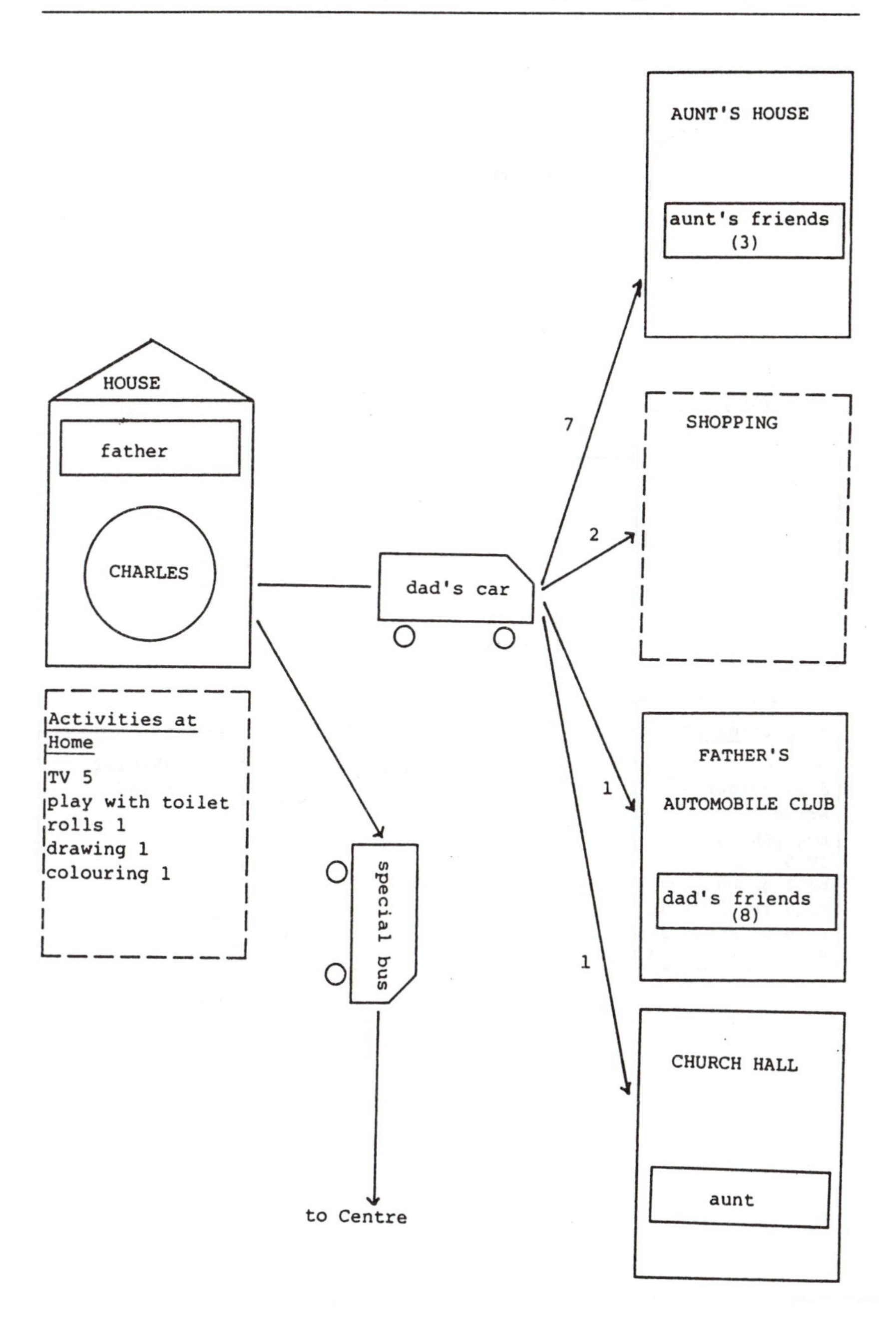

Figure 4.7 Charles – second monitored fortnight at home (1986)

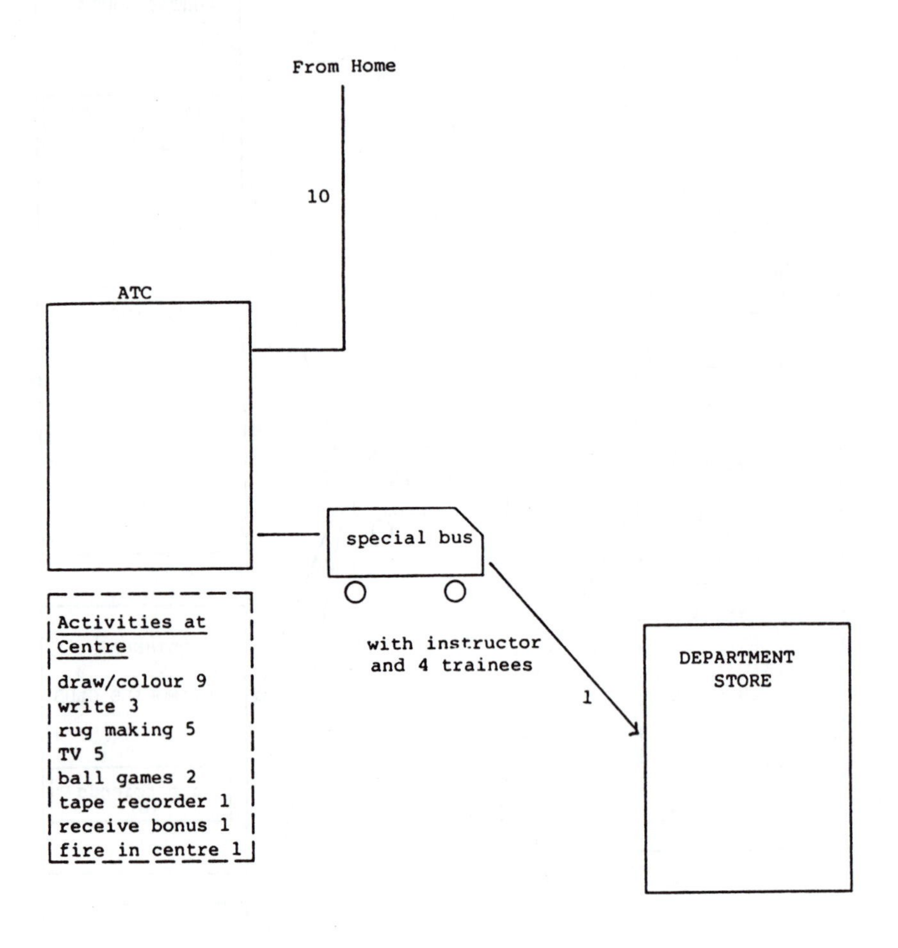

Figure 4.8 Charles – second monitored fortnight at the centre (1986)

1986

Let us now move on another year to the second monitored fortnight. The home network is shown in Figure 4.7 and the centre network in Figure 4.8. At home there were no significant changes except perhaps that Charles was now drawing and colouring at home as well as at the centre and that his domestic activities at home were not recorded. For example, during the first monitored fortnight there had been reference to items like dressing and cleaning teeth. These were, by the time of the second monitored fortnight, activities taken for granted and not worthy of mention.

At the centre (see Figure 4.8) Charles was still spending a great deal of time drawing and colouring, doing craft work, engaging in discussions and so on. This, however, is from the point of view of Charles himself. We asked him, with his father, to recall the activities each day he had undertaken them. We can compare this with the full list of activities as seen by the staff:

Activity	*Objectives and Comments*
Social skills: [*++] Letters and words. Name and address identification. Time and measurement.	To be able to understand basic concepts. He will say he understands when he doesn't. You wonder whether you're progress is so slow, you start doubting yourself. Too many people at too many different stages in the group
Discussion group[+]	To get him to join in. Can easily be disrupted. Getting him to think and make decisions. To stimulate his imagination
Games (free choice)	Socialising
Disco+	Socialising
Television (free choice)[+]	Socialising
Role play[++]	Make him aware of reality. He doesn't always join in

Craft work (free choice)	To make a decision about what was important to him, e.g. numeracy, time. This arose because an outing was cancelled. He decided to do his name and address. I was pleasantly surprised he decided to do this
Outing[+] shopping in the town and cafeteria	Seeing a world outside the ATC. His world is mainly indoors. Another trainee is inclined to baby him. He is quite happy to be looked after by her. Another objective was to help him to make decisions as to what to buy. The bus was cancelled and a part of the outing plans had to be dispensed with. Trainees had to cope with a disappointment. This made him realise you have to pay for things dealing with money. We were very rushed. You run out of places to take them to
Audio visual,[++] job/work 'nature under the sea' discussion	To stimulate conversation – sometimes he is reluctant to talk. To be aware of the world around him. One member of the group dominates the discussion and can be disruptive. Sometimes there can be boredom. This is dependent on the choice of programme. You feel you are not getting anywhere. Charles would like to sit and colour in all day. Trainees as a whole enjoyed the film about human growth. (It was pointed out that there was a link between the audio visual programme, the outing and the discussion group.) 'You begin to wonder what you're really getting

	out of the outing – what you've originally planned; the assessment etc. – what does it mean when you've actually got ten people around you?'
Craft work. Rug hooking	Colour. (He tends to isolate himself.) Counting (he won't tell you if he's made a mistake). Creative skills (different stages of trainees can be a problem). To encourage him to communicate with others doing similar things, such as to pass colours, ask for help, to socialise
Personal hygiene: shaving	To improve shaving and nail care; shoe polishing

Key: * – Major activity, i.e. at least two full days or equivalent during monitored period

** – Main activity, i.e. at least half the time during the monitored period

+ – Activity described as 'very important' by staff

++ – Activity described as 'crucially important' by staff

The comparison between centre activities and objectives between the first and second monitored fortnights reflects a number of changes that were taking place while the research was in progress. The manager described these as 'a more purposeful approach based on trainees' needs'. It was the intention to develop assessment procedures.

At the end of the research period we asked (at home) what progress Charles had made. This was set out under headings as follows:

Activity	*Progress since first monitoring*
Helping at home (or managing on his own at home)	No progress. But he will water the plants
Recreational activities	I don't know. He is going to be in the tug of war team
Social activities and mixing with others	He has always been good at that
Basic education	No progress known
Communication with others and general confidence	He is speaking better

In answer to the general question of whether the father could think of anything specific that Charles had learnt he said he could not pinpoint anything but there was no doubt his speech was clearer, and he thought this was because of the speech therapy he had had.

1988

After the research was completed we went back to ask what changes had taken place at the centre, or were planned. We were told the centre had perhaps become more outward looking. Three clients had started on a work experience scheme funded by the European Community. There were plans to extend the scheme to establish a further education course and residential accommodation for clients outside daily travelling distance of the centre (this would not apply to Charles). A centre café was now operated by clients. A hairdresser visited and gave classes. Horse riding was now an additional activity. Some clients were involved in a YMCA keep-fit session. The manager said she had applied for an additional staff member as an outreach family worker. This would be to encourage clients to improve skills in order to move into alternative accommodation or to use their skills to stay within their own families if this was appropriate.

1995

Charles's father died and after moving briefly to stay with his aunt he was admitted to a 24-hour staffed house run by a housing association on the outskirts of the city. The project also provided minimally supported flats and, after a year spent in the main house, Charles moved to one of these flats where he now stays with another tenant. He continues to attend the same centre and the following details of his life were given by him for the purposes of this book.

He does his own washing and housework, makes his breakfast and weekend lunch, including his own packed lunch for eating at the centre. He does these things independently but gets support for a main meal as well as for shopping. When shopping, he chooses his own clothes to buy. He uses local 'over the counter' shops and can manage to transact business himself at the post office. He travels independently on public transport to reach the centre.

Charles' interests include watching television, and visiting the local pub, community centre, and the library. He goes to discos with friends and volunteer workers. He also belongs to a country and western club in the city centre. He has holidays both in this country and abroad. For a time, Charles was on the tenants' committee.

Charles said his old friends and relatives keep in contact. His aunt visits him weekly.

At the centre, the staff told me Charles is doing a refresher course on independent travel to enable him to visit his aunt on his own and to enable him to develop his own circle of friends. He also has support from the centre in budgeting for shopping. He is allowed a sum to do his shopping and the goods purchased are brought back to a flat (with 3 others) in the centre where he prepares a meal, with support.

He goes out from the centre to bowling at a local sports centre as well as attending indoor hockey. He spends two half days away from the centre with staff at his own flat. He also has support using his local library.

The policy of the centre has further developed since 1988. The emphasis is now on support rather than training and on doing activities outside the centre, using community facilities and volunteers, rather than staying in the centre.

POINTS FOR DISCUSSION

1. Compare the home situations of Freddy, cared for by his mother and Charles, cared for by his father.
2. The aim of this centre was seen in 1986 as being to develop people's potential and perhaps particularly to enhance the quality of life at home and in the community. What do you consider to be Charles' particular needs in this respect? In other words, how do you assess the quality of his life at home and in the community?
3. Do you think that Charles was too protected at home? If so, in what ways?
4. Do you think enough attention was being given to Charles' possible feelings towards the death of his mother? What would you expect his feelings to be? Is there any evidence of what his feelings were? Is it the role of the centre staff to cope with such issues? If so, how?
5. Charles is described as introverted. Presumably, we are all either introverted, extroverted, or some combination of the two. The question may be, whether whichever tendency we have, is so extreme as to cause difficulties in daily living. Is there any evidence that this is the case for Charles?
6. We have in this material a detailed description of the expectations of staff in relation to particular activities and also frank expression of the feelings staff had about their task. Charles' key worker at the centre feels he has not enough time to give the individual attention which would otherwise be rewarding to Charles and from time to time he even wonders how much the attempt to individualise, without the time, is worthwhile. If you were the centre manager, is there anything you could suggest (for example using room management techniques) which would resolve this issue for staff and help Charles? (Room management is a system allowing two or more staff to have different roles in a larger group, for example allowing one to concentrate on management and interruptions while the other concentrates on the educational interaction.)

7. Charles seems to want to spend a lot of time colouring but the staff seem slightly uneasy about this. Have you any ideas for making more of this as an activity? (e.g. in terms of what he could be colouring, or what he is colouring for).
8. Underlying the above and some of the other questions is perhaps the feeling that all that can be done for Charles is to occupy him – and that sometimes this is all Charles wants. What is your reaction to this suggestion? If Charles is 'happy' should he be left alone?
9. Towards the end of the material an account is given of changes that occurred at the centre since the research ended. How might these changes have benefited Charles? What is the evidence in the final update (1995) that there were benefits? How much might these benefits be attributed to the centre's new policies?

SOME GENERAL POINTS FOR DISCUSSION

1. Comparing the networks in these two cases, assess the role of the centre in meeting client needs.
2. Compare the quality of communication between the client and the centre in each case.
3. Comment in each case on the extent to which centre practice activities are: a) focused and b) co-ordinated in meeting client needs.
4. Assess the extent to which the centre forms part of a planned programme with other agencies in delivering a 'package of community care'.

CHAPTER FIVE

Contrasting Patterns of Living and Contrasting Services

1985

Jeffrey and Jane were both 16. They had cerebral palsy. They had epileptic fits. They were severely physically disabled and could only get about in a wheelchair. They had profound learning disabilities. Their support needs are described below:

Activity	*Jeffrey*	*Jane*
Dressing	He needs to be dressed	Lifts her arms for dressing. She has to wear special suits
Toilet	When taken to the toilet he is now always ready to perform	Doubly incontinent
Eating	Can eat food by himself using spoon. Needs some physical assistance but this is decreasing daily. Seems to be better at centre	Uses spoon and fingers to feed herself. She is supervised to ensure she doesn't put too much on her spoon
Mobility	Wheelchair. Now sitting up on his own. He can roll over and move himself.	At home: can crawl; can move around on the floor on her bottom

Activity	*Jeffrey*	*Jane*
Speech	Can express dislike of things. Makaton is being taught	Brain damage affecting speech. She will stop action if you say 'no'
General	Has screaming tantrums – can last several minutes,but generally happy. His views are obtained by interpreting gestures, smiles etc. Has no sense of danger	A happy person most of the time but will sometimes start rocking her head back and forth or banging with a stick. Knows about dangers of fire
Progress	More concentration, less screaming tantrums. Feeding has improved. He is more responsive	Each year she progresses a little – e.g. no problems with bowel movements now

Both Jeffrey and Jane had problems in self-management skills and neither could accomplish any of the more sophisticated 'daily living' skills such as travelling on their own, understanding money, or cooking a meal for themselves. They had multiple disabilities. Having said that, they had their own individual personalities, likes and dislikes. Jeffrey liked watching football. Jane liked being mischievous and when she was crawling she tried to play with ornaments at home and, if she could, she would break them. The mother thought that she knew what she was doing and was deliberately mischievous.

JEFFREY

Jeffrey was the eldest of a family of five and lived in a council house on the outskirts of a small country town. An aunt and cousins lived on the same estate.

Figure 5.1 shows Jeffrey's network of contacts from home in 1985. It is an example of an 'embracing' network – that is to say the family reached out to embrace all that was available in the community and had a large network of friends and relations, as well as social services (Seed 1990). They maintained contact with the pre-

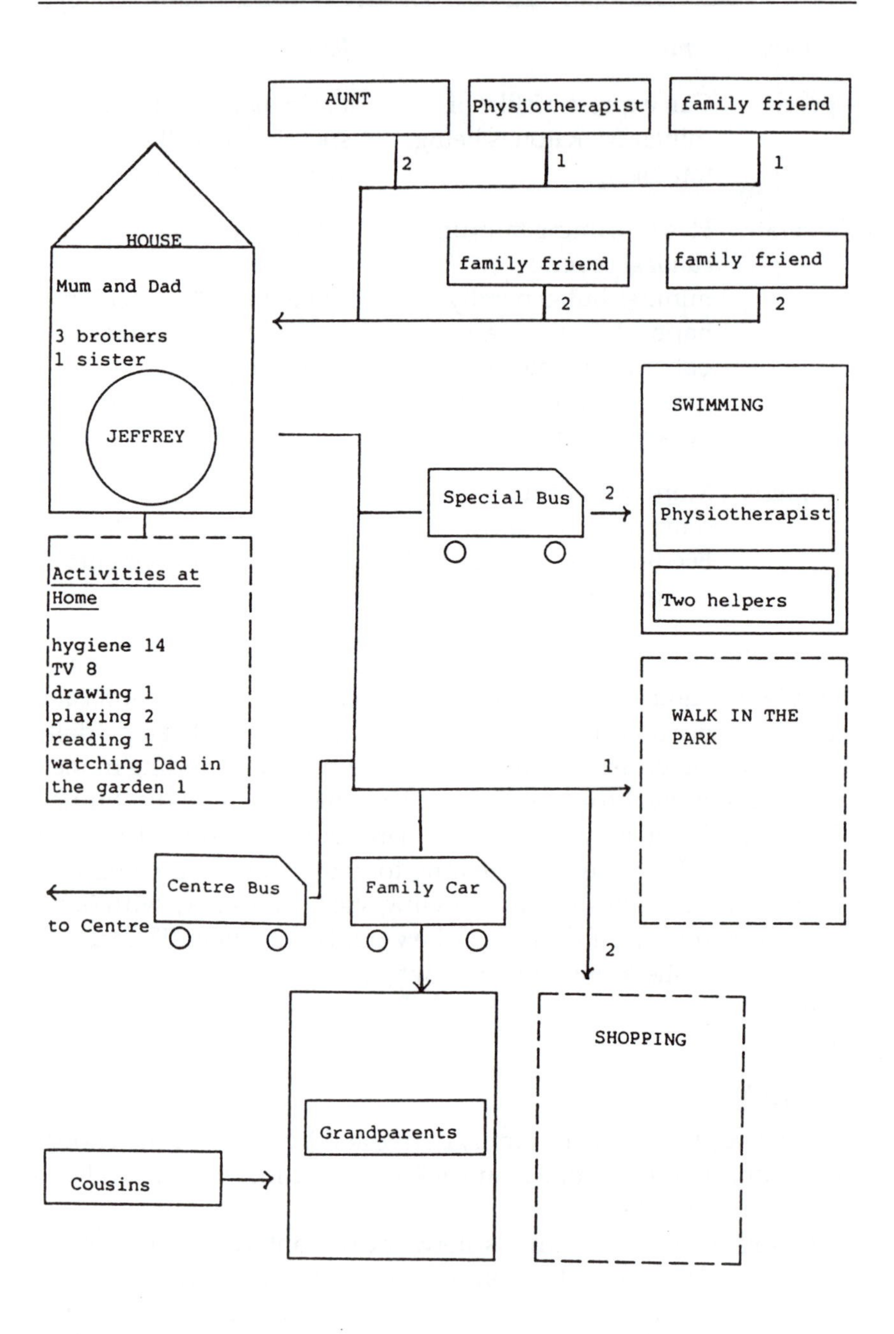

Figure 5.1 Jeffrey – first monitored fortnight at home (1985)

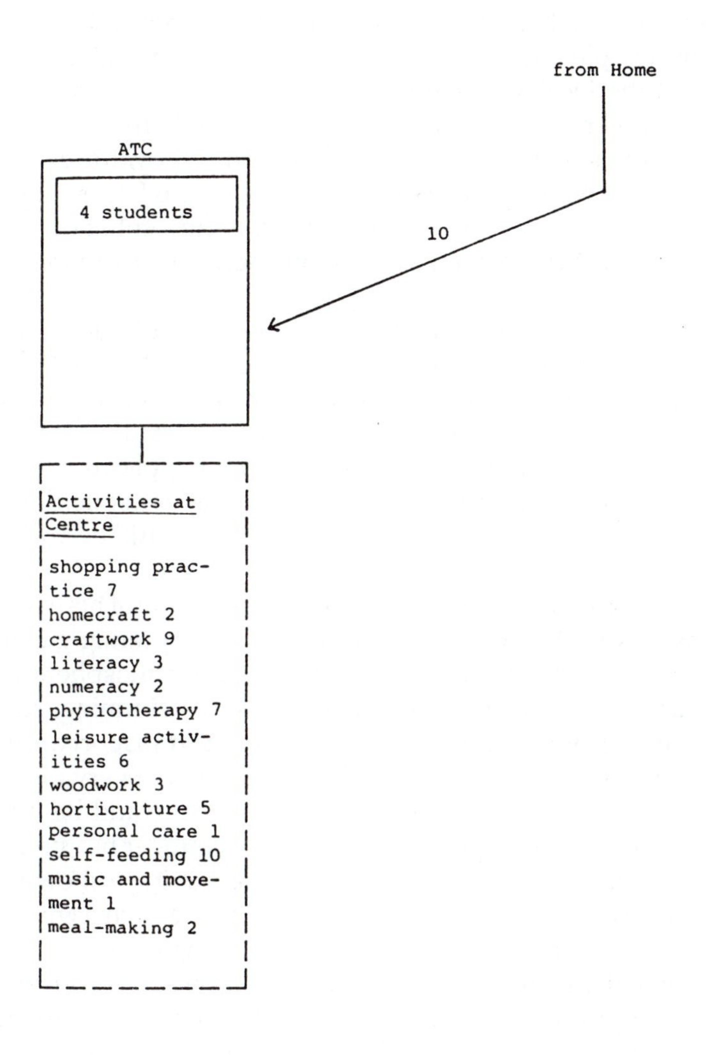

Figure 5.2 Jeffrey – first monitored fortnight at the centre (1985)

vious school and Jeffrey on one occasion got a lift home from one of his old teachers. He was excited about this. They were conscientious in going to hospital to attend to Jeffrey's foot following an accident. People who were important ranged from relations and friends to the local shopkeeper and volunteers at the swimming pool. Wherever they went as a family they took Jeffrey with them. Some family activities were centred around Jeffrey, for example, 'walks' in the wheelchair to the local park where Jeffrey enjoyed watching football. Despite his disabilities, Jeffrey got about in his wheelchair including taking part in a sponsored walk organised by a social club.

Another typical feature of an embracing type of network was that while the parents were appreciative of the services they received, they were anxious to improve them. Thus the mother took the initiative in getting the local authority to install a radio telephone link in the minibus – in case anything happened to Jeffrey at the centre. This was important because he was epileptic. She also suggested to me (the researcher) that a section should be added to the centre for respite care, for example, at weekends.

Jeffrey himself was far from being passive. In spite of his inability to speak, I was able to obtain his views by interpreting gestures, smiles etc. He particularly appreciated the warm atmosphere at the centre, and amongst centre activities, he liked swimming, riding, gardening and outings. He also appreciated the transport arrangements. I thought this was a good illustration of how very disabled people can, with patience and skill, communicate and be understood. At home, Jeffrey played a lot with his younger brothers and sister and a major event (see Figure 5.1) was having a shower. He also practised standing, using a standing frame. Otherwise, like many others, his favourite activity was watching television.

Jeffrey had attended a special unit in an ordinary local primary school. The physiotherapist Jeffrey had at school still maintained contact and visited. Why did Jeffrey move to a day centre when he could have stayed at school until 18 or 19? Partly it was because the family lived near a new purpose-built centre based on an educational model where education from school could be continued. Moreover, he could mix at the centre with young adults rather than with primary children. The mother, however, had some initial misgivings about whether Jeffrey might be too young. She said he was not used to adult company 'all day'.

The parents visited the centre before Jeffrey started and staff visited the family at home. The mother was particularly impressed that the manager phoned on the first day to tell her how Jeffrey had got on. The mother's expectation was that they would teach Jeffrey social skills and that he would make new friends. She also felt he would, at least, be occupied. She would also gain in terms of respite because the centre had shorter holidays than the school.

Jeffrey had a key worker at the centre and his view was that the centre should aim to provide social education and, where appropriate, preparation for employment. For Jeffrey the aim was greater independence as well as giving respite to the family. The educational approach was very broad concentrating, in a structured programme, on developing Jeffrey's physical, mental, emotional, social and sensory potential. The activities were those which would be appropriate for any 16-year-old person. In no way was Jeffrey treated as a child. Staff objectives and comments related to some of the activities will illustrate this (during the first monitored period):

Activity	*Objectives*	*Comments*
Meal making	That Jeffrey will participate in making his own lunch, reacting to smells, noises, textures, tastes	Jeffrey seemed more interested
Horticulture	To play with leaves and flowers, to smell scented leaves	He tore leaves and flowers into small pieces. He was happy
Leisure activities	To let him reach and play musical equipment	He liked different sounds of music and watching others play pool. He was happy
Shopping	For Jeffrey to react to items in the store and to his surroundings	Jeffrey is always delighted to be outdoors. He enjoyed carrying items on his tray

Activity	*Objectives*	*Comments*
Physiotherapy	Independent control	He did very well within limitations. He went from being cheerful, then sad, then cheerful again. He noticed when people ignored him

A lot of the activities had an assessment element. It was important to establish exactly where Jeffrey was in a range of different surroundings with different kinds of stimulation.

1986

By the time of the second monitored fortnight a year later there was perhaps more emphasis on following objectives through. For example:

Activity	*Objectives*	*Comments*
Social skills	To recognise when he needs the toilet and indicate this	This is related to a pattern of toilet training for future independence
Physiotherapy	To maintain the present extent of his physical flexibility	
Basic education	The focus currently is on education teaching him to concentrate and to develop eye contact	
Home craft	To extend use of hands and to participate as a member of the group	

Activity	*Objectives*	*Comments*
Horticulture	To experience activity which may not be seen as 'ordinary' acts for most wheelchair people	
Pottery	Stimulation. To increase sensory awareness	
Community project outside the centre	To introduce him to new areas, broaden his horizon, to see more of the world. To let the world see more of him.	
	Language stimulation through surroundings	

These were only a few of the activities listed.

What was achieved? Recognising that progress is slow, it was noticed at home that recreational activities had led to an improvement while at the centre he was initiating contact more. His feeding had greatly improved. It was noticed both at home and at the centre that he was better able to concentrate and that he had less screaming tantrums.

Jeffrey was seen in 1986 as a good example of:

1. An excellent fit between activities at the centre and the kind of life and ambitions a young person with multiple handicaps is able to have at home.
2. A demonstration of the viability of an educational approach, instead of simply 'caring and occupation' for someone with such profound handicaps.
3. An illustration of the principles of normalisation to people with severe handicaps.

1988

In getting permission to use this material I was also able to update what had happened since 1985. Progress had continued and amongst the specific points made by the mother were the following:

- A special adaptation at the centre had enabled Jeffrey to use the computer. He loved it.
- He was about to go to his second disco, arranged by the centre but not held there. Other people without learning disabilities took part.
- Self-feeding continued to improve. Diaries kept by the centre revealed that he fed himself with no one at hand. It was arranged that the mother should go to the centre to see this for herself. He had since fed himself at home too. The mother recognised that Jeffrey was 'having her on' in pretending that he was unable to feed himself.

JANE

1985

Jane lived with her mother and father in a private house on a main road in a residential estate. She had two older brothers, one of whom had left home. The mother who had the main burden of looking after Jane said that the elder brother used to help. His help was missed particularly since Jane had become heavier as she had got older and she had to be lifted out of her chair up three concrete steps to get into the house. Moreover, the bathroom was upstairs. Mother recently strained her shoulder in trying to lift Jane. She said they were hoping to build an extension to the ground floor for a new bathroom and toilet.

Jane's home-based network is shown in Figure 5.3. It is typical of the type we call 'self-contained'. Such networks are typically restricted and there is suspicion of the world outside. During two monitored fortnights Jane's only visit out from home was a weekly 'walk' in the park. Although not featuring during these fortnights, there were, according to the mother, two other significant people in Jane's life: the doctor and the priest. She had a social worker whom, she said, did not visit (presumably at the mother's request) because 'I am independent'. On the other hand she wanted, and

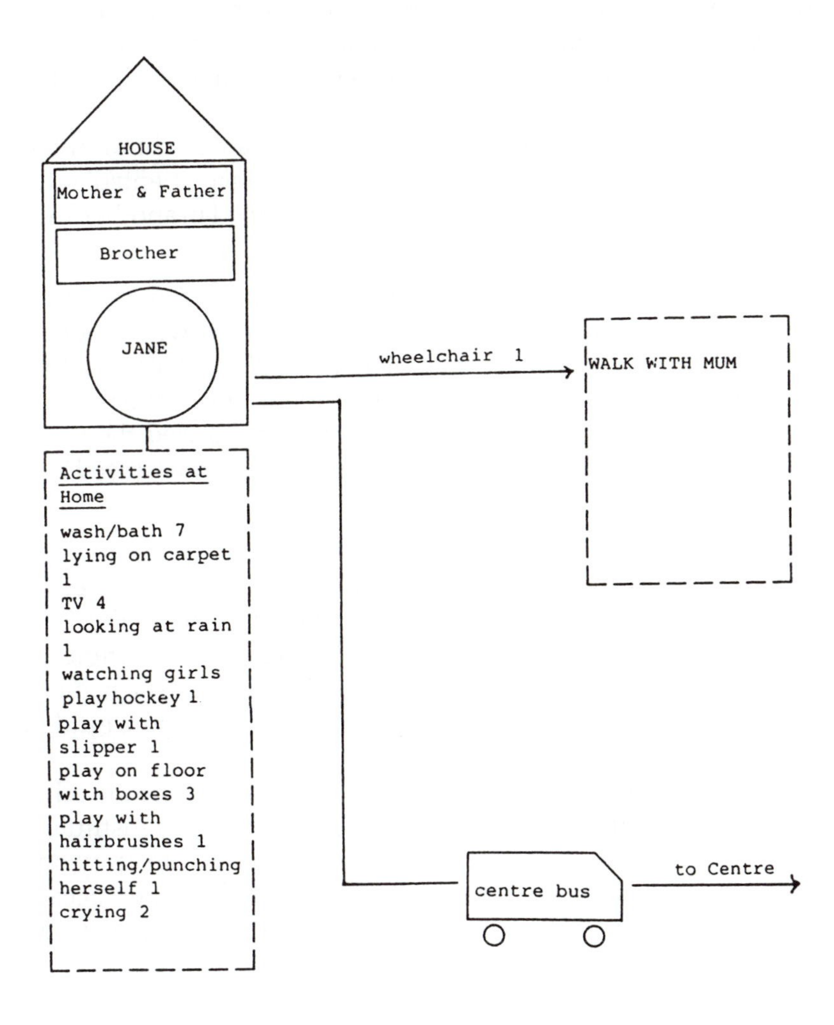

Figure 5.3 Jane – first monitored fortnight at home (1985)

needed, the social worker's involvement in arranging respite care when the mother had to go to hospital. The mother complained that it was only within a week of her going that she had heard from the social worker that arrangements had in fact been made to admit Jane to a home run by a voluntary society. She had to push for these arrangements.

Some parents looking after profoundly disabled children tend to be what we have called in our research 'handicap oriented' rather than 'family oriented'. The distinction is described in another study as follows:

> The families can be said to fall into two main groups. Firstly, there are those who wish to be involved in what could be called 'the world of mental handicap'... Secondly, there are...parents who resisted the idea of becoming too involved with other parents and who instead emphasised their commitment to a normal life for the family as a whole. (Seed 1988, pp 69–79)

Jeffrey's parents were 'family oriented' in that Jeffrey was involved in a wide range of family activities which were not just centred around his own needs. In Jane's case, however, the mother's life was very much centred around Jane's disability. For example, she had twice taken Jane to Lourdes. During the research she had been prepared to take Jane into her bed at night because she would not settle.

As with Jeffrey, Jane's mother had a positive view of the school she had attended. This was a special school. They had instituted a toileting programme which they wanted the mother to carry on at home. However, the mother said she had had to give it up because it was so difficult to lift Jane up the stairs. The mother said that while Jane was often happy, life had its grim moments. The mother's diary recorded:

> As Jane is profoundly mentally handicapped, things or events do not change much from day-to-day. At times she gets frustrated, possibly the reason is that she is unable to talk or walk. She tries to hit herself, slapping her face. She tries to bang her head on the floor. It is very upsetting for me.

On another day she was causing her mother 'a little upset with behaviour – trying to bang her head on the floor – continually laughing'.

The mother had various complaints about the centre – for example, transport. She described this as 'very bad'. A van picked Jane up around 8.15 am. There was only room for two wheelchairs so 'I have to lift my daughter up three deep steps and place her on the seat'. By the second monitored fortnight, a year later, the position had improved.

The centre Jane attended was some distance away and the mother hoped that she would be transferred to a new centre very close when this was available. If the mother wanted to visit the centre it entailed two bus journeys.

The mother was interested in what was going on at the centre and she compared the centre unfavourably with the school in terms of information conveyed through diaries. The school had always sent a diary home on a day-to-day basis. The centre had a policy of returning diaries on a weekly basis but this did not always happen. The mother was prepared to say that probably the centre 'don't have enough staff to cope' and maybe this was the reason.

Another 'loss' in moving from school to centre was the absence of a physiotherapist. Neither, according to the mother, were there any visual or hearing tests which she had come to expect as a result of experience at special school. Why, then, had Jane transferred from school to centre at 16? The mother explained she could have stayed longer at school but she was afraid that unless she took up a place when it was available she might not be able to get one.

Nappies were another matter which concerned the mother. The school had provided nappies which were very good ones. They changed colour on a tape marker when Jane needed changing. The centre, on the other hand, had asked the mother to provide pads herself. The mother complained that clothes were not always returned from the centre and these were an expensive item. Jane's centre did not have the same educational orientation as Jeffrey's centre had although clients were called 'students'. Like Jeffrey's centre it was purpose-built but it was larger and people, like Jane, with profound disabilities were more often confined to a special care unit. The following are some of the activities and objectives given by staff during the first monitored fortnight.

Activity	*Objectives and Comments*
Tea and toast	To eat and drink without supervision. Expectations are over a long term. There is little day-to-day improvement
Floor work stimulation	Response to stimulation. Limited response. Persistent stereotyped behaviour, distraction
Swimming	Stimulation in water. Expectations are over a long term and show little day-to-day improvement
Table top play (putting coloured rings on plastic cones, building on plastic blocks, etc.)	Did not expect a good result. Jane did a lot better than expected. She possibly remembers the exercise from school. She has varying moods from very happy to self-inflicted pain
Exercise to see if she would use her wheelchair under her own power	Expectations were high because she was offered cake and juice as bait/reward. She loves food
Disco	None. Free playtime
Outing to the park	Expected Jane to enjoy the outing. She did enjoy it but not as much as expected. She went into a bad mood – started to hit herself on the legs. After some time she became happy again
Messy play and musical movement	Not much response expected as this was the first time this activity had been undertaken. She played with the sand but ignored everything else. With the music and movement she was okay. Her behaviour was hard to describe. She was in a poor mood and would often burst into tears

1986

By the time of the second monitored fortnight the mother reported that relationships and communication with the centre had much improved. In the summer especially there were more outings from the centre. For someone as restricted as Jane at home in terms of outside contacts, the contacts from the centre were important.

While the mother had criticisms of the centre she was extremely grateful for the respite it offered. It allowed her to do shopping and 'gives me a break'. On the other hand, she had anxieties for the long-term future. She wished there was somewhere where 'I knew for certain she should go to in order to relieve the burden'.

1988

In obtaining permission to use this material the mother modified her complaints about the centre. Transport was now 'quite good'. Diaries were much better and she was getting more information. She added that 'soft therapy' was now being done at this centre and in general activities seemed to be better, giving more opportunity for working on a one-to-one staff:student basis for Jane. However, the mother was still looking forward to the possibility of Jane attending the new nearby centre which was due to open soon. She said she had not yet heard whether Jane would get a place there. On the question of the incontinence pads, the mother said she was now getting these through the clinic but there was a problem obtaining the correct knickers for the pads.

To summarise the contrasting patterns of living for Jeffrey and Jane: Jeffrey engaged in a wide range of activities many of which would be regarded as appropriate for someone aged 16. Jane, on the other hand, lived a much more restricted life. Jeffrey was frequently reported to be happy whereas Jane appeared sometimes to be very unhappy.

How do we account for these differences? We will find an answer, perhaps, in looking at the attitudes within the family, the opportunities available in the home-based networks, and in the way the expectations of parents, in Jeffrey's case, were matched by the attitudes, expectations, and opportunities found at the centre.

Jane's need for greater opportunities appears only to have been addressed several years later at a new centre.

1995

If one had been predicting future opportunities in 1988, one would have anticipated further advances for Jeffrey. However, as we shall see, much depends on how different centres have been able to develop new policies in the face of increased demand and limited resources.

JEFFREY

Jeffrey's parents told us Jeffrey was still attending the same centre, but new arrangements had been introduced whereby the premises had to be used for another client group one day in the week. People with learning disabilities attended a different building on this day, but Jeffrey was unable to attend because there was no access for his wheelchair. He therefore was allowed to continue to attend his regular centre, with another wheelchair user, but was not allowed to meet or mix with the other centre users. One must assume this extraordinary arrangement reflects overstretched resources.

His mother did not feel Jeffrey had made any substantial progress at the centre, though he still enjoyed going and especially enjoyed the swimming. The two members of staff who had mainly been working with him had now left.

An unsatisfactory situation where the only residential placement was in a hospital had not yet been resolved, although other alternatives had been explored. Again, wheelchair access had been a problem.

The parents had found a caravan site for weekend use where they took Jeffrey.

Jeffrey's brother had married and left home.

JANE

In 1990 Jane moved to the new centre which had opened nearer to where she lived and which could better provide for her special needs. Meanwhile, an extension was built onto her house where she remains living with her mother. She is said to be looking 'fine and healthy'. Her key worker reported that she was receiving hydrotherapy and physiotherapy. She was not 'stuffing her food in the way she used to'. Attempts are being made to provide additional home support as well as a befriender to take her out in the evenings. I was told there was no evidence of father being any more involved in looking after Jane.

POINTS FOR DISCUSSION

1. Compare Jeffrey and Jane in terms of their support needs and consider their different personalities, i.e. what sort of people are they?
2. What does age-appropriate treatment mean for Jeffrey and Jane? They were aged 16. Could they in all respects be treated like people of that age?
3. What are the arguments for and against a young person with severe learning disabilities leaving school at 16 or staying on at school until 19?
4. Compare the experiences of Jeffrey's parents and Jane's parents with regard to the transition from school to centre.
5. Both purpose-built centres had special provision for people with severe and profound learning disabilities. Jeffrey was fully integrated with other clients. Jane was kept apart during much of the day. Which approach do you prefer? What are the staffing implications?
6. Jeffrey's centre was based on an educational approach. Was this approach vindicated?
7. Compare the different patterns of living at home for Jeffrey and Jane. In either case what, if any, would be the appropriate involvement of a social worker? Can you suggest suitable social work aims?
8. If Jane's mother was reluctant to receive a social worker in the home, what could the social worker do about this?
9. Does one accept that some parents will be more 'family oriented' and that others will be more bound-up with the lives of their disabled member? What are the implications?
10. In Jane's case, the researcher's contact was with the mother. We hear nothing about the father. How can Jane's father be helped to become more involved? Compare this with Jeffrey's situation where the father was very much involved.
11. How could the parents of Jeffrey and the parents of Jane be helped in enriching the lives of their disabled son and

daughter at the same time as they maintained and developed their own lives? What additional support was needed in each case?

12. What steps could a social worker, or worker from the centre take to help to develop and extend Jane's home-based network?
13. Are centres adequately equipped to provide for the practical needs of people with profound disabilities and to make it easier for parents to cope at home – e.g. in relation to appropriate transport, clothing, play equipment, bathing and toileting equipment, educational equipment etc.? In the last ten years a number of small specialist centres for people with profound and multiple disabilities have been opened. What is your view of this possibility as an alternative to 'special units' within larger centres?
14. What do you think of the practice of daily diaries between centre and home? What should be the purpose of such diaries? Who should write in them?

A third example of a young person with multiple disabilities is Richard (Chapter 6).

CHAPTER SIX

Respite

Respite features prominently in parents' expectations of what centres should provide. Yet it does not often feature as a main aim of centres so far as management is concerned. Is there a conflict here? If centres focused exclusively on the respite needs of carers would this inhibit the development of policies and practice aiming to develop the client's independence and integration into the community?

The severity of the disability is not the only factor determining the extent to which parents need respite. Some other factors which are of key importance were listed in Chapter 2. In more detail, the following factors are taken into account in considering respite needs:

- the extent to which the client's behaviour makes demands on parents or other carers
- the extent to which the disability has particular implications in terms of constant attention and anxiety, e.g. someone prone to epileptic fits
- the home situation, e.g. whether it is a single parent household where the caring function cannot be shared with another adult
- lack of available support from the extended family
- family isolation, especially where there is no private means of transport and lack of access to public transport.
- parents' or other carers ill health or disabilities
- where the parents or other carers have more than one disabled person dependent on them

- where parents or other carers are at work. This is of increasing importance today with the larger share of the labour market being taken up by women in part-time employment, which in some cases can follow similar hours to times when a centre is open.

Some of these factors apply to many, if not most, of the cases discussed in this volume. In this chapter we are concerned with situations where not only one of these factors but several apply and where the need for respite appears to be extreme and paramount. Is this fact incorporated in the thinking and planning of what is available at day centres? If not, do the parents or other carers get an adequate respite service from other sources?

PETER

1985

Peter was aged 25 when the research started. As well as having a severe learning disability, he suffered from epileptic fits and hay fever. His younger brother, aged 18 was, in the parents' view, even more disabled. He has Down's syndrome. Their grandparents live locally and, as will be seen from the network for the first monitored fortnight, (Figure 6.1) featured in the families support network. I (researcher) described the mother as 'managing to battle her way through years of administrative red tape', as she tried to provide the best services for both her sons. Despite being told by a doctor when Peter was four years old that he would need to go to school as soon as possible, it took the mother three years to get an offer of a special school place.

She was dissatisfied with this particular special school as she felt that Peter needed the stimulation at a higher level. By insisting, she eventually ensured that he was offered a place in an alternative school, conditional on his being there for just one year only. At the end of this period he was moved to a private special school but the transport arrangements became too much when the second disabled child was born. He was then placed in a junior occupation centre which was where the local authority had originally offered him a place when he first reached school age.

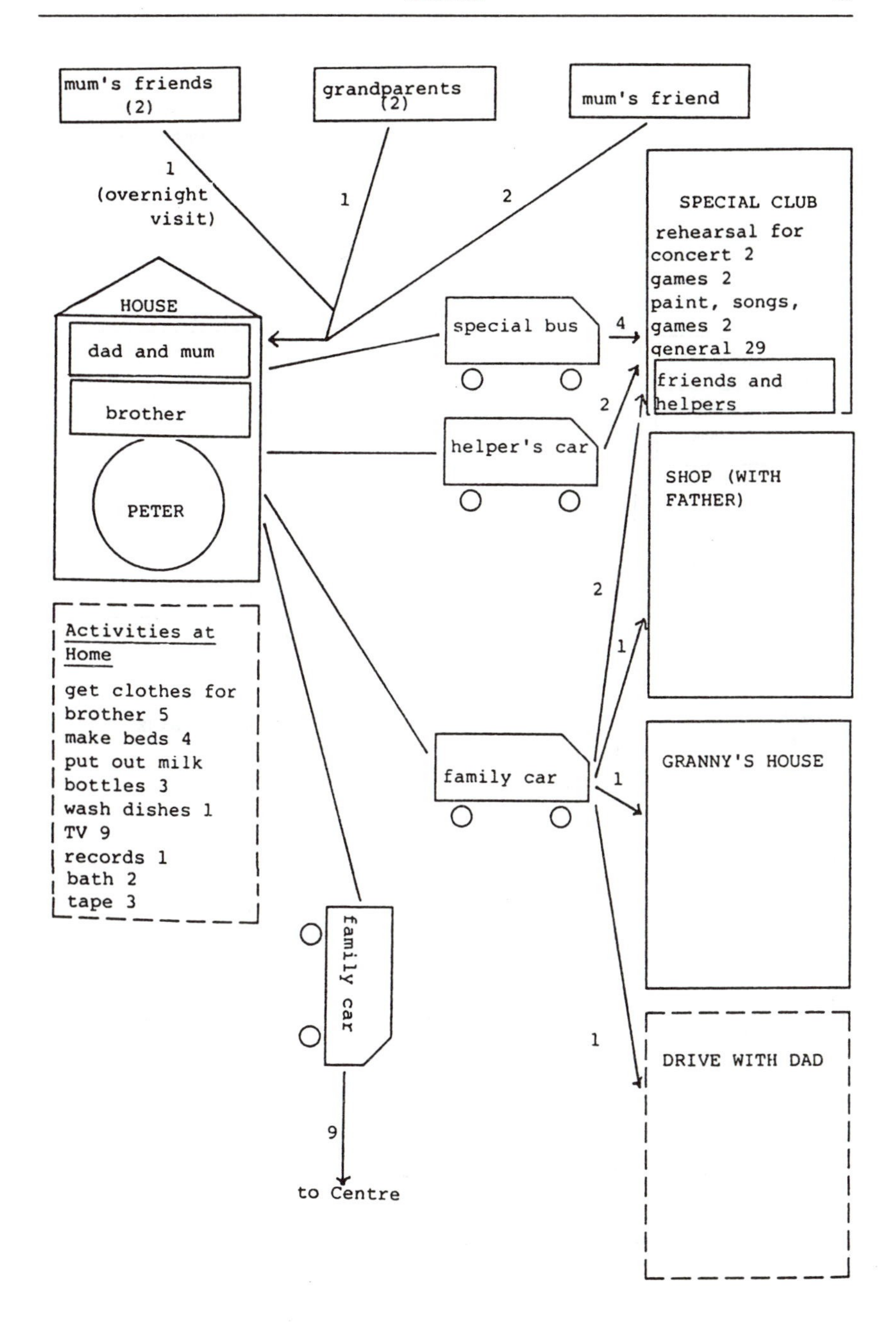

Figure 6.1 Peter – first monitored fortnight at home (1985)

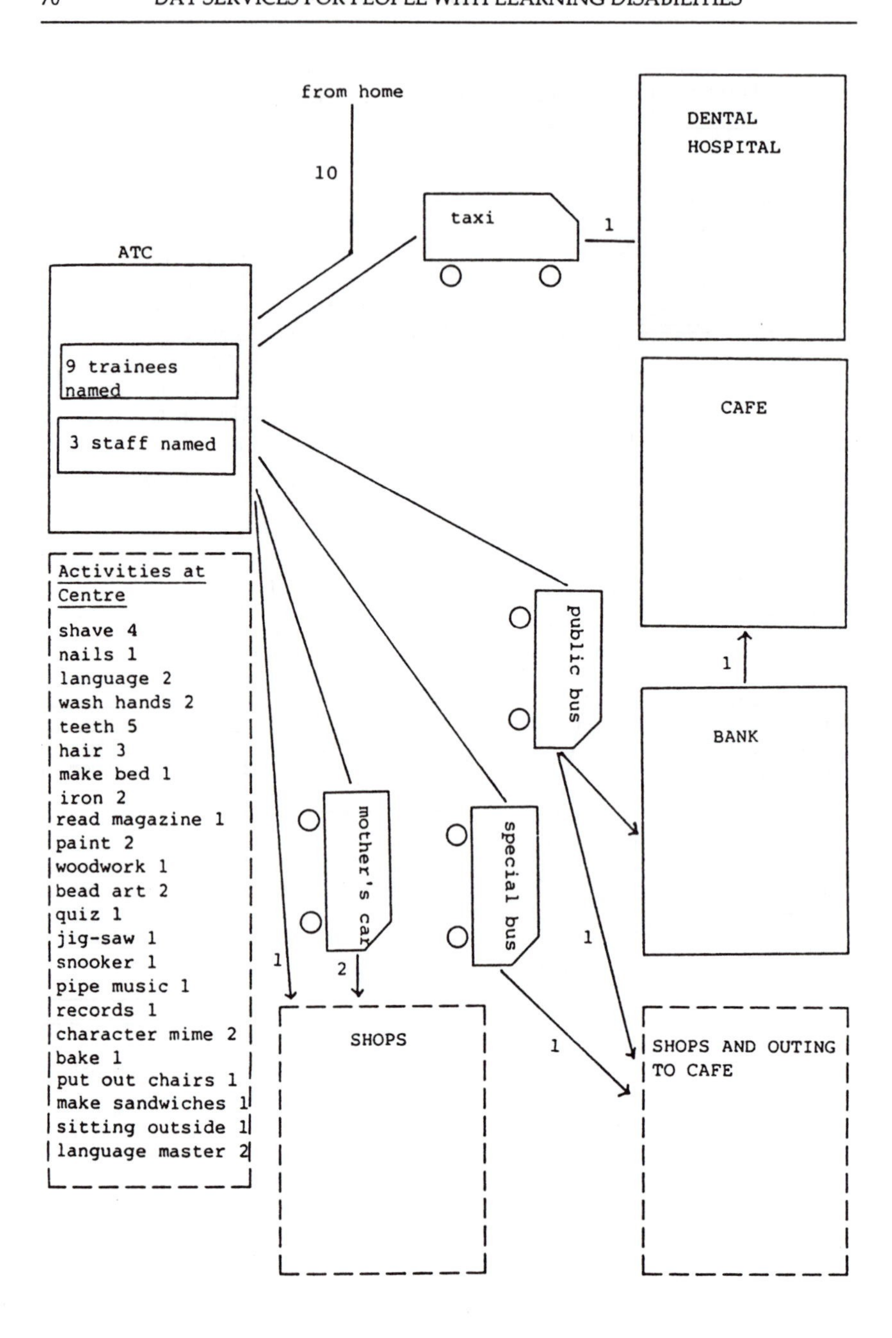

Figure 6.2 Peter – first monitored fortnight at the centre (1985)

I would describe Peter's home network as 'embracing' (See Chapter 5) in that the mother was anxious to reach out to take advantage of every possible opportunity for help and support. She fought (and won) the opportunity to attend reviews at the centre.

However, the mother was particularly concerned that (residential) respite care places were not sufficiently or readily available. She pointed out that she and her husband had not had a holiday together, separate from their two sons, for 20 years until eventually the authorities arranged for the younger brother to get a residential fortnight at the same time as Peter was going on holiday with the centre. Yet the mother foresaw a problem in the future because the brother's respite facility was officially only intended for children. What residential respite care place, she wondered, would be available when he was transferred to an adult training centre in the near future?

The mother was critical of the social work department for not providing a regular visiting service. When the research started, the mother said that she had seen a social worker four months previously. The social worker was supposedly finding out about whether Peter could get respite care, as he had previously had at school. Over a year later the mother said that she had had one visit from a social worker in six months and she commented, 'If they've withdrawn her (from the residential respite home) they should have told me.' In contrast, she said that the health visitor she had had some years ago had been 'super'. She had popped in regularly advising on such practical issues as incontinence and giving new information. She said this health visitor had died. The social worker had never given the same kind of support.

The mother pointed out that respite in this situation had two aspects. The parents, particularly the mother, needed a break. Things were easier since the father especially took early retirement to look after his two sons. The mother said she now feels she has a lot more energy. The second aspect of respite concerns Peter himself. He needs a break from his parents.

The aims of the centre, as the mother perceived them, were to offer respite for Peter in terms of a changed environment where there would be more stimulation than he can be given at home. In talking, early on in the research, about changes that had occurred at the centre the mother said that when Peter first went they did rug making and joinery 'which were really too advanced for him'. She preferred it now, because there are more domestic skills being taught.

The mother benefited from her sons being at school (during term time) and at the centre because 'it allows me to get on with shopping, appointments etc.'. She also used her free time to 'pop in to the centre every day'. It will be seen from the network diagram (Figure 6.1) that the mother took Peter to the centre by car.

Before we consider in detail what happened at the centre, we will look at Peter's support needs.

Activity	*At home (Parent's view)*	*At the Centre (Staff view)*
Dressing	Needs help in putting clothes on correctly, e.g. buttons and laces are still difficult	Needs someone, for example to fasten a jacket zip. If it is started at the bottom then he can do it up. He needs his shoelaces tied and buttons undone
Wash, bath and toilet	He needs someone there because of the epilepsy. He can manage most things except washing his hair and brushing his teeth	Washes hands and face after a fashion. Cannot wash hair or get dried after a bath. He can run water satisfactorily but needs help in washing in the bath (at the end of the research it was noted that due to father having retired there was more time at home to let him try to do these things for himself)
Eating and drinking	No problems	Needs help in drinking cutting up meat as he twists the knife round the wrong way

Activity	*At home (Parent's view)*	*At the Centre (Staff view)*
Mobility	No problems	No problems
Preparation of food and drink	Makes an attempt to butter a slice of bread. Epilepsy is the problem in using a cooker. He can fill the kettle – it makes him feel important	Has a little difficulty holding a knife to butter bread. He could put the contents of a tin into a saucepan. He would need supervision in making toast – there's always someone there anyway but possibly he could do this himself. (At the end of the research it was noted that he could now break an egg and mix ingredients with his hands though sometimes eggshell fell into it)
Household tasks	Makes his own bed. Can use vacuum cleaner – very careful with plugs. Uses the carpet sweeper. He is very proud of being able to make his bed	He can make his bed. Can sweep floor though not perfectly. Has never been tried with vacuum cleaner. He can plug in an iron and switch a washing machine on and off
Use of money	He knows you need money to buy things with and knows the difference between needing a large amount of money and a small amount of money	No understanding

Activity	*At home*	*At the centre*
Communication	He can make basic needs known, e.g. needs the toilet or drink of water but it is difficult for others to understand him. He uses his own gestures. We tried Makaton but we found he had his own gestures and it was confusing for him	This is his main problem. Using his gestures we can understand him and we're trying to get him to vocalise. A stranger couldn't understand. (At the end of the research period it was stated he had come on in this area)

We will now look in detail at the objectives for each of the specific activities undertaken at the centre (during the second monitored fortnight).

Activity	*Objectives and Comments*
Trip to supermarket to buy food for holiday+	To be able to identify sugar, milk, etc. (He cannot go to the shops often at home as mother also has his brother who is disabled to look after). To learn where the things in the kitchen come from
Gardening+	Enjoyment. To help him overcome his reluctance to get his hands dirty. This is improving
Cleaning windows (combined with other domestic tasks)*+	Enjoyment
Simple woodwork	Manual dexterity
Simple puzzles	To learn about colours and shapes. To concentrate. Also observation (assessment)
Domestic: iron articles; put out plates and cups for lunch. Madehimself a cup of coffee*++	To learn to manage more independently. to be able to help
Attempted writing	Basic steps in education

Activity	*Objectives and Comments*
Out for a walk	To learn how to conduct himself in public
Language+	To improve communication
Went to park and public building++	To make him aware of the outside world (new experiences)
Domestic: helped tidy up, and made cake. Set table for tea bread*++	To learn to look after himself and develop independence skills
Used the language master+	To improve communication
Listened to records with other trainees (disco)+	To give trainees free choice on Fridays
Painting (Peter's choice)	Opportunity to exercise choice
Went to local shops for a paper++	To be aware of the world outside
Cutting out from magazine and using the shape as a stencil to make a copy picture for mum	Encourage dexterity
Game of bowls	Enjoyment
Holiday – away from centre+ (holiday period commenced at the end of the monitored fortnight)	Opportunity to be away from his parents. Seeing new situations e.g. gardens, statues, cafés. Enjoyment

Key:
* Major activity, i.e. at least two full days or equivalent during monitored period
** Main activity, i.e. at least half the time during the monitored period
+ Activity described as 'very important' by staff
++ Activity described as 'crucially important' by staff

Several things can be noted from these activities. First, there is evidence of an awareness by staff of the situation at home, including positive features such as the fact that the father, being retired, now had more time to be with Peter at home. Second, some activities were deliberately introduced in order that they could be further developed in the home situation.

Third, there was an effort to enhance opportunities in the community, recognising that the mother was tied down because she had another son with learning disabilities.

In summary, therefore, we can say that the situation was one where the mother knew what she wanted from the centre, and that the centre appeared to be aware of this and able to respond. Respite was not simply viewed as giving a break to the mother but of taking advantage of the opportunities that were available when a break was provided in a positive way. As a result, it was intended that when Peter and his parents were together the opportunities for Peter's learning and development would be enhanced.

1986

The following progress was recorded:

Activity	*At home*	*At the centre*
Helping at home and managing on his own	Progress – filling a kettle and making beds. Switching television on and off. Making sure everything is off at night	
Recreational activities	Concert at Thursday club. Joining in well with football	Keen but doesn't, for example, run for a ball
Social	At Thursday Club – progress joining in with others	More alert and involved
Basic education	A little improvement – seems to have got away from the pattern of writing 'P's all the time. He now writes 'R's and 'D's	

Activity	*At home*	*At the centre*
Communication and improved general confidence	A little improvement in general. No progress in communication	Confidence due to better health. Has come on in his communication

1988

In getting permission from the mother to use this material she told us that special care respite was now available but it was in the country and she thought there should be a respite facility for people with severe disabilities in the locality, or at least nearer their own home. She also told us that there had been rumours that the centre Peter attended, which was a small one, might be closing in favour of attendance at a larger centre.

Because she was anxious about this she made enquiries and was told that there was no intention to close the centre where Peter now attended. She also told us that the social worker had still not visited.

1995

The centre Peter attended did, in fact, close and Peter was transferred to a more modern, purpose-built centre. Day service policies also changed in favour of more emphasis on individualised attention. A community service volunteer had been able to assist. We were told that Peter had responded and developed to a point where the parents were prepared to accept that the centre programme should be challenging to Peter – and not merely provide respite.

POINTS FOR DISCUSSION

1. Although Peter attends the centre everyday he does not spend the whole of the day at the centre. Discuss the activities outside the centre and their relevance to Peter's lifestyle at home.
2. What do you understand by 'respite'? Is this the main function of a day centre? Answer this question firstly in general terms and then with particular reference to Peter and his parents

3. Does the emphasis on respite in this case in any way inhibit other objectives which might be appropriate for Peter's development?
4. What difference does it make to the situation that the father is now retired?
5. Discuss the particular needs and problems that arise from someone who, in addition to having a learning disability, is prone to epileptic fits?
6. Consider the comments made by the mother about the absence of a social worker regularly visiting her at home.
7. In what way can the service provided by the centre be linked more closely with the services that could be available from an area team of social workers in this case?
8. Peter's mother was anxious about the possibility of the small local centre closing. Where centres may seem vulnerable to closure, how should parents' anxieties be dealt with?

RICHARD

1985

Richard, aged 17, had cerebral palsy and multiple disabilities. He was described as quadriplegic. He also had severe and quite frequent temper tantrums. Richard's mother had died some years ago and before that his parents had separated. His father was still alive and from time-to-time Richard's sister had met him in the street. On such occasions he asked after Richard but did not make any contact. Richard now lived in a ground floor flat with his sister and a nephew. The family previously lived in a rural community but they moved into a city in order that there should be better facilities and also more tolerant neighbours. There was a history of neighbours complaining about Richard's temper tantrums and the noise he made where the family used to live before. It was a relief to the sister that the neighbours did not appear to complain where they now lived.

On various counts this was a situation where the need for respite featured prominently. The responsibility of looking after Richard

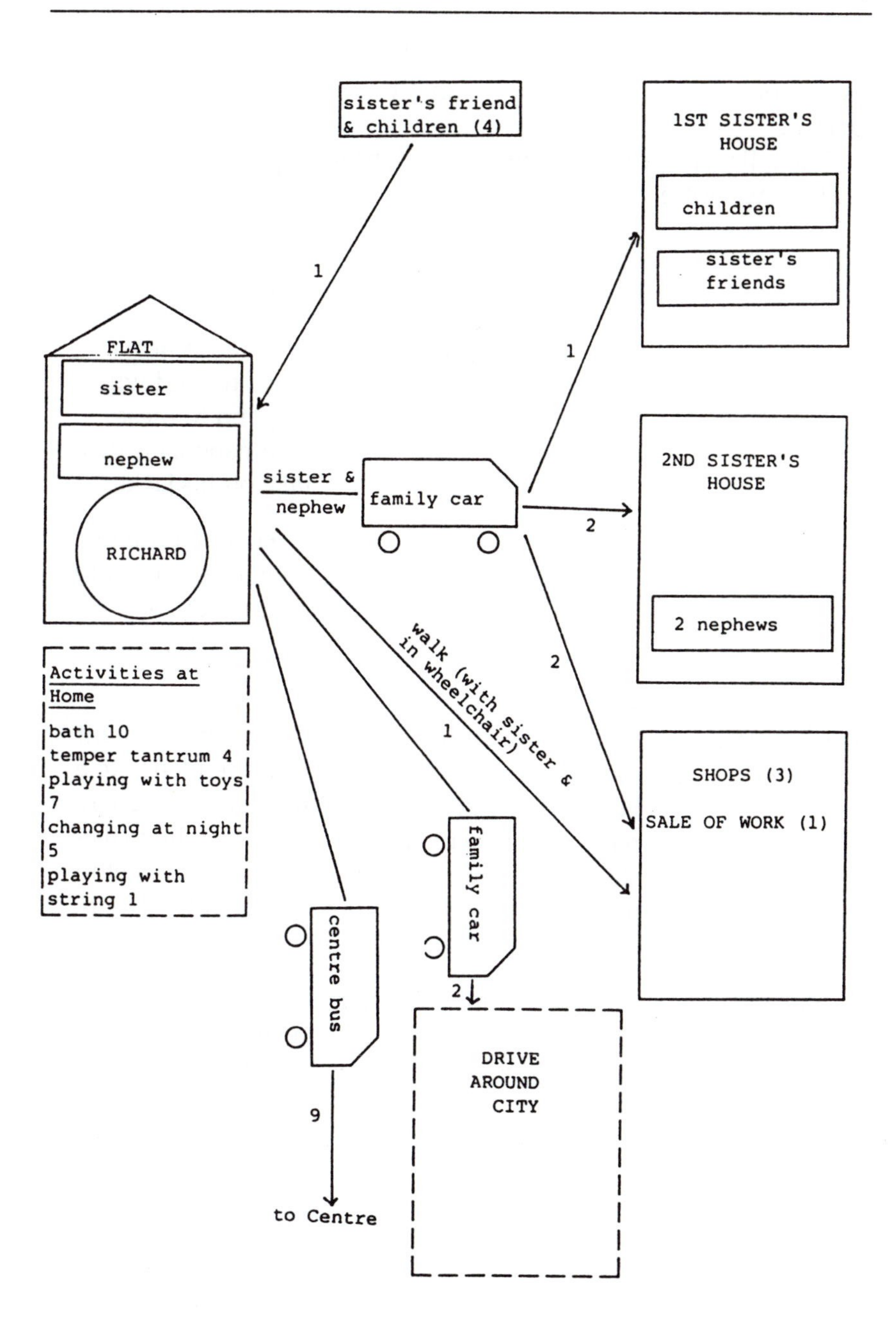

Figure 6.3 Richard – first monitored fortnight at the centre (1985)

was one which was both exceptionally demanding and which fell exceptionally on one person – namely his sister – who is not his parent.

The following are the details of Richard's support needs at home and at the centre:

Activity	*At home*	*At the centre*
Dressing	Will lift his arms up to be dressed (that is all)	Will lift his arms, stand up and will respond to these commands. He can take off his jacket He will raise his own arms without a command, i.e. if engaged in taking jumper off
Wash, bath and toilet	Has temper tantrums. Due to bowel problems, he uses incontinence pads. Needs help at all stages. His sister is often up at night to change the sheets	Doubly incontinent. Has a tendency to a rash due to rubbers. With help he makes an attempt to get in and out of the bath
Eating and drinking	Can eat by himself with a spoon and drink from a cup. Food is cut up small for him	Can eat by himself using a fork and spoon and drinks from an ordinary cup. Food is cut up for him

Activity	*At home*	*At the centre*
Mobility	Can walk from house to the bus waiting outside. Cannot manage stairs	Just very lazy – can walk short distances. Will sit down in the middle of the street. Manages to walk from bus to centre in the morning
Communication	Can express choices, e.g. relating to food and make basic needs known to sister only. Cannot express choices about where to go	Will cry if upset. Can respond to simple requests. Cannot express choices otherwise. He will reach out a hand if you are passing with a drink

All of the above support needs relate to self-care tasks. There was only one reference in the data we collected relating to daily living tasks. This was a reference to the fact that at the centre he could pour himself a drink although 'he may make a mess'.

Richard had no effective use of speech. His sister had recently discussed this with his general practitioner who said that his vocal chords were destroyed so that he could not learn to speak. However, he had been heard using words at home. His sister said that on one occasion he said 'Mamma' and on another day he said, 'Allow' (hello). He could not repeat these sounds, however. The sister would like to take Richard to a speech therapist to explore this further.

While concerned about the possibilities for Richard's development, the sister's initial expectations of the centre were that it should provide respite – respite primarily for herself but also respite to Richard himself in giving him a break from home. The sister described her feelings when Richard got a place as 'relief'. She said: 'The centre is a blessing, a lifeline. I don't know whether I'd manage to go on with Richard at home 24 hours a day. For example, how will I get the washing done?'

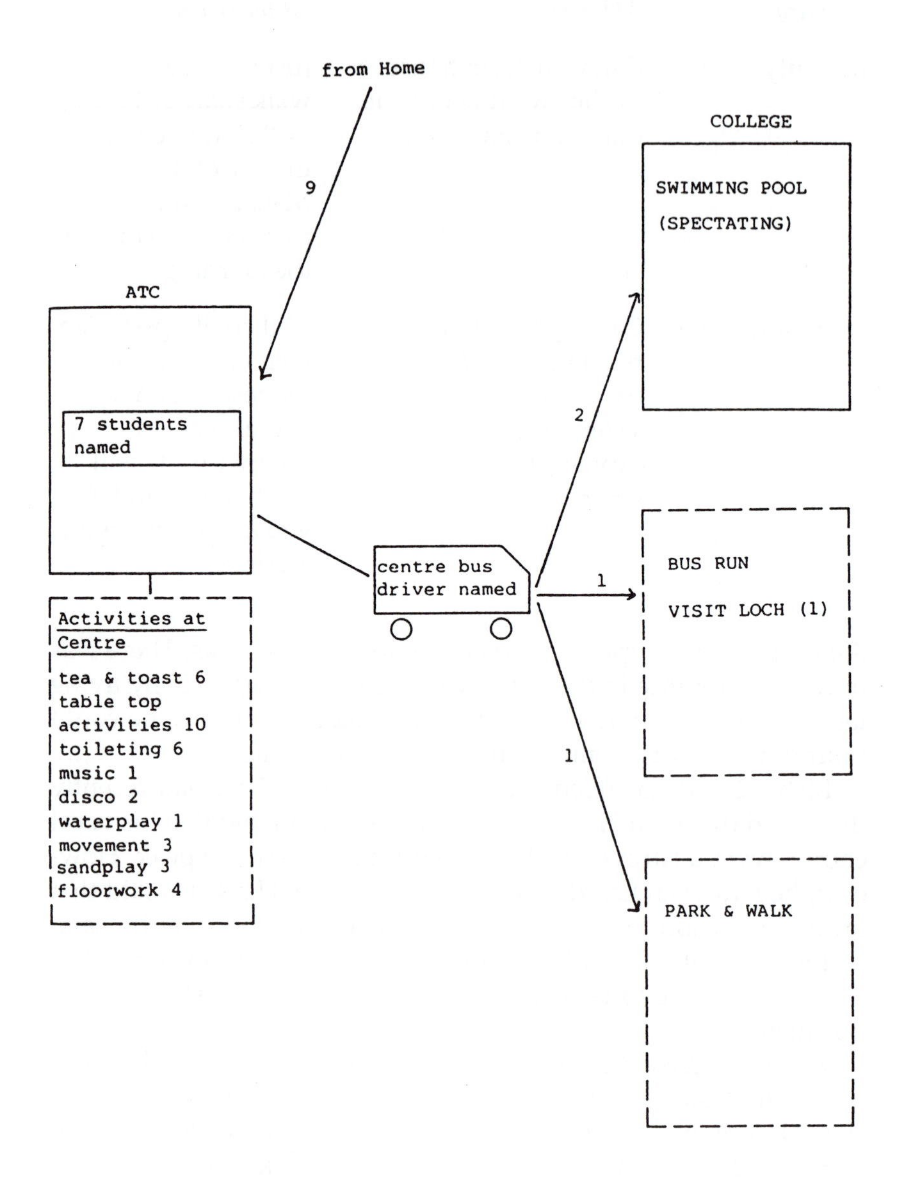

Figure 6.4 Richard – first monitored fortnight (1985)

Additional respite was available from other sources, however. A respite project took him from home for a weekend every two to three months allowing the sister to 'sit back and relax for the weekend'. At the start of the research period she also had one evening every month to herself when a registered voluntary home care worker came from the community centre. During the research period this arrangement ran into difficulties because the person concerned was now doing overtime at his own job. The community centre were hoping to find another person and in the meantime, the sister commented that she also had help from another sister in the family. Visits to this sister's house are shown during the monitored fortnight (see Figure 6.3).

The instructor who was the key worker at the centre was more modest about the role of the centre in providing respite. He acknowledged that it provided respite 'to a limited extent' although he said this was not the aim. He saw the aim of the centre rather in terms of social education, 'preparing trainees to survive in outside life, removing them from the sheltered existence that is their usual role; emotional development and improving their self-image'. The instructor thought that contacts with the carers at home were important and that the diary system which they use at the centre was too impersonal.

When the research started a parents' meeting had been held as an alternative means of communication. Richard's sister had been invited but she could not, in fact, attend.

Richard's activities and staff objectives during the first monitored fortnight at the centre were as follows:

Activity	*Objectives and Comments*
Swimming	Play in water. He doesn't appear to like water and resists participation in play
Toileting	It is expected that he will be wet or soiled
Tabletop activity	To play quietly unsupervised
Movement	To allow himself to be moved
Floor work	To co-operate in activities
Outing	No objective stated

Activity	*Objectives and Comments*
Tabletop play – putting geometric shapes into correctly shaped holes	As expected he would not do anything unless he was given a lot of prompting. He did not seem to be in a good mood. This was probably because he was continually soiling his pads, which usually happens a couple of days every month
Walking exercises	He does not like to walk more than 10 to 20 steps at a time. Better than expected – he walked around the centre once every half hour
Outing to the park	Trying to get Richard to walk as far as possible. He walked a lot further than usual. Being pushed in the wheelchair was used as a bait. His mood changed from good to bad to good when he was in the park. He was in a very happy mood when he came back to the centre

The general comment from the key worker at the end of one particular day was that Mary (another instructor) had a lot to do with getting Richard to walk more: 'He seems to get along better with women than men, possibly because he stays with his sister, who is able to control his moods to some extent.'

The researcher observed Richard at the centre and commented:

> Richard is in the profound disability unit. His key worker is George. George said there is no particular person at the centre whom Richard turns to and George sees himself as being authoritarian towards Richard. By this he means that he does not pamper him in his moods. George is in direct contact with Richard for about half the day but not always on a one-to-one basis. This would be in the unit, in the messy play area or on the stage doing exercises. I have observed George persisting with Richard in working with the exercises despite Richard's very vocal protests.

> From my own observations Richard tends to be a loner. He does not initiate contact with trainees or staff (except through tantrums) and is not one of the profoundly disabled trainees whom the other trainees choose to help.
>
> Much of the time he rocks himself, sitting cross-legged on a chair and it is difficult to get him to make eye contact. During a party at the centre he sat with his two sisters all the time, rocking and holding a toy. He was smiling sometimes and looking happy. The deputy manager stopped to speak to him at one stage. His sister told me that at the centre he had been having a lot of problems with more frequent tantrums recently. Later I was told he had to be taken away from the party into the unit because of a tantrum. His sister stayed with him during this tantrum.

Apart from the staff at the special unit, other important people in the centre network would have been the driver and the woman escort on the centre bus (see Figure 6.4). They helped him get on and off and he also travelled on the centre bus for outings. If the bus was late in the morning Richard got anxious and this was expressed when he started rocking impatiently.

Richard has not had as much attention in his life as some others with cerebral palsy would have had. He was not brought up in an area where there were special facilities. For a while he had no schooling. Although the sister's first concern was for respite at the centre there were signs towards the end of the research that she was becoming increasingly concerned that Richard's potential should be developed. We have already referred to her concern about speech therapy, which was not available. (Compare the opportunities offered in the case of Jeffrey – see Chapter 5.)

1986

During one home visit, the researcher asked the sister whether anyone had ever been to advise her about Richard's temper tantrums. She said she had been to see her general practitioner about it and he had put Richard on drugs during the day to try to calm him down. This had partially been successful but he was still having temper tantrums 'now and then'. She wondered whether it was worth getting in touch with the general practitioner again. Meantime, at the centre, by the end of the research the key worker felt there had perhaps been some improvement. He felt that possibly his bowel movements were now more regular. He was less frequently hanging his head. He laughed more and was 'much cheerier'.

Richard spent a lot of his time both at home and at the centre playing with toys. His key worker was critical of some of the toys that were available for people in Richard's situation. He described the equipment as 'age-inappropriate' – e.g. children's toys for adults. He said, 'I do not think manufacturers make available a range of equipment adequate for adults – equipment for students to sit on to spread their legs may have childish faces painted on it. I would be embarrassed for visitors to see me using such equipment with adult students.'

1988

In obtaining permission to use this material we received a letter from Richard's sister saying that Richard still loved going to the centre. The sister herself had been very ill last year and had been diagnosed as diabetic and was having to inject insulin twice daily. She said she was 'now keeping fine'.

1995

Richard's care needs indeed proved too great for his relatives to cope with and he has been moved out of the area and into residential accommodation.

Meanwhile, this centre's policy has radically changed in the past few years, with more focus on individual assessments and training programmes. Had he stayed, it is likely the features of his training activities – for example, playing with toys, would have changed. But whether this could have enabled Richard to stay at home is not clear.

POINTS FOR DISCUSSION

1. On what grounds is there a particular need for respite to be provided in this case?
2. How does the respite role of the centre relate to other respite facilities available?

3. Compare the respite role of this centre which offers full-time attendance with Freddy's situation where centre attendance was only part-time (see Chapter 4).
4. How would it have affected the home situation in this case if attendance had been part-time rather than full-time?
5. How does respite relate to other objectives at the centre?
6. Do you think the centre fulfils the objectives stated for it by the key worker, i.e. in terms of social education and preparation for 'survival'?
7. Apart from the facts of Richard's disabling condition, in what ways has he been at a disadvantage in his life? Answer this question with regard to: (a) services; (b) neighbours and social contacts; (c) opportunities for education and training; (d) understanding of his condition and circumstances.
8. Is there any other evidence that anyone has ever tried to understand, as opposed to simply trying to control, Richard's temper tantrums? What factors do you suppose could contribute to these? In answering this question, try to put yourself in Richard's place and imagine what it must feel like.
9. There is no regular visiting social worker in this case. Is it reasonable to expect a social work role to be fulfilled by a key worker from the centre? If so, suggest what additional work the key worker should be undertaking. If not, suggest what tasks a field social worker should be undertaking in relation to the work undertaken by the key worker at the centre.
10. How might the arrangements for assessment and care planning, since 1993, have affected the management of this case had they been in place in 1985?

CHAPTER SEVEN

When Carers Become Older or Die

WHEN CARERS BECOME OLDER

What is the role of a day centre for adults with learning disabilities when carers at home are getting older? In the first set of two examples, Anne and Joe, we consider this question together with the more general issue of whether people with learning disabilities should move (and, if so, when and where to?) before the people they depend on for support at home are themselves no longer able to cope without increased support. In the first case, Anne, the carers are the client's father and his housekeeper. In the second example, Joe, the carers are two his sisters.

ANNE

1985

Anne is nearly 40. She could be classified as having a severe learning disability. However, any such general classification could be misleading. It would cover up the wide differences in Anne's abilities in different kinds of situations. For example, while Anne cannot handle money in the sense of being able to go into a shop, select the correct money for articles when she does not know the price beforehand, and check the change afterwards, she can add up sums in an exercise book. She can read and write to a limited extent, and sufficient for normal daily living. She completed parts of her own diaries for the research. Yet she has problems with toileting (on account of a physical complaint) and she could not prepare, by herself, a simple meal.

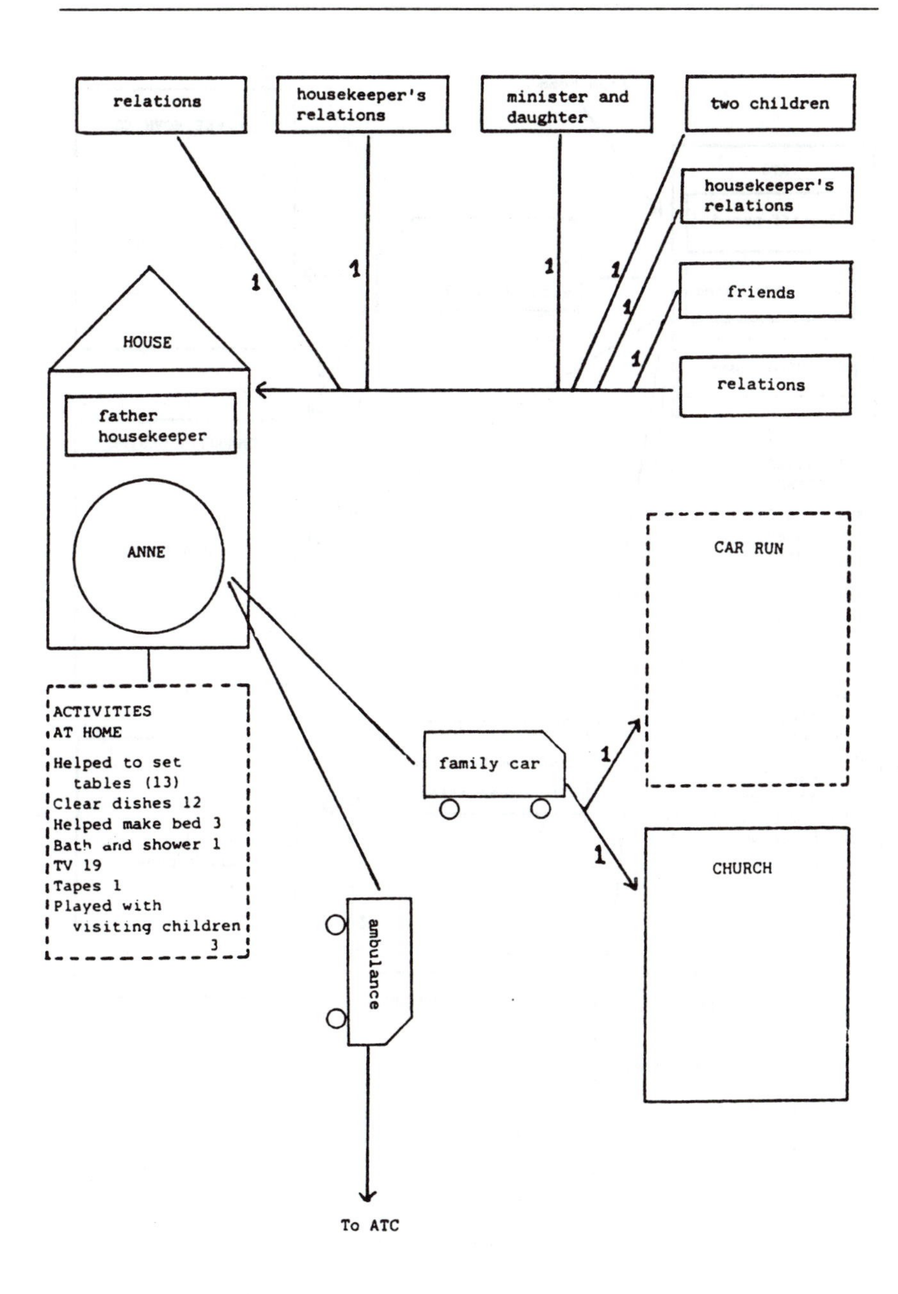

Figure 7.1 Anne – first monitored fortnight at home (1985)

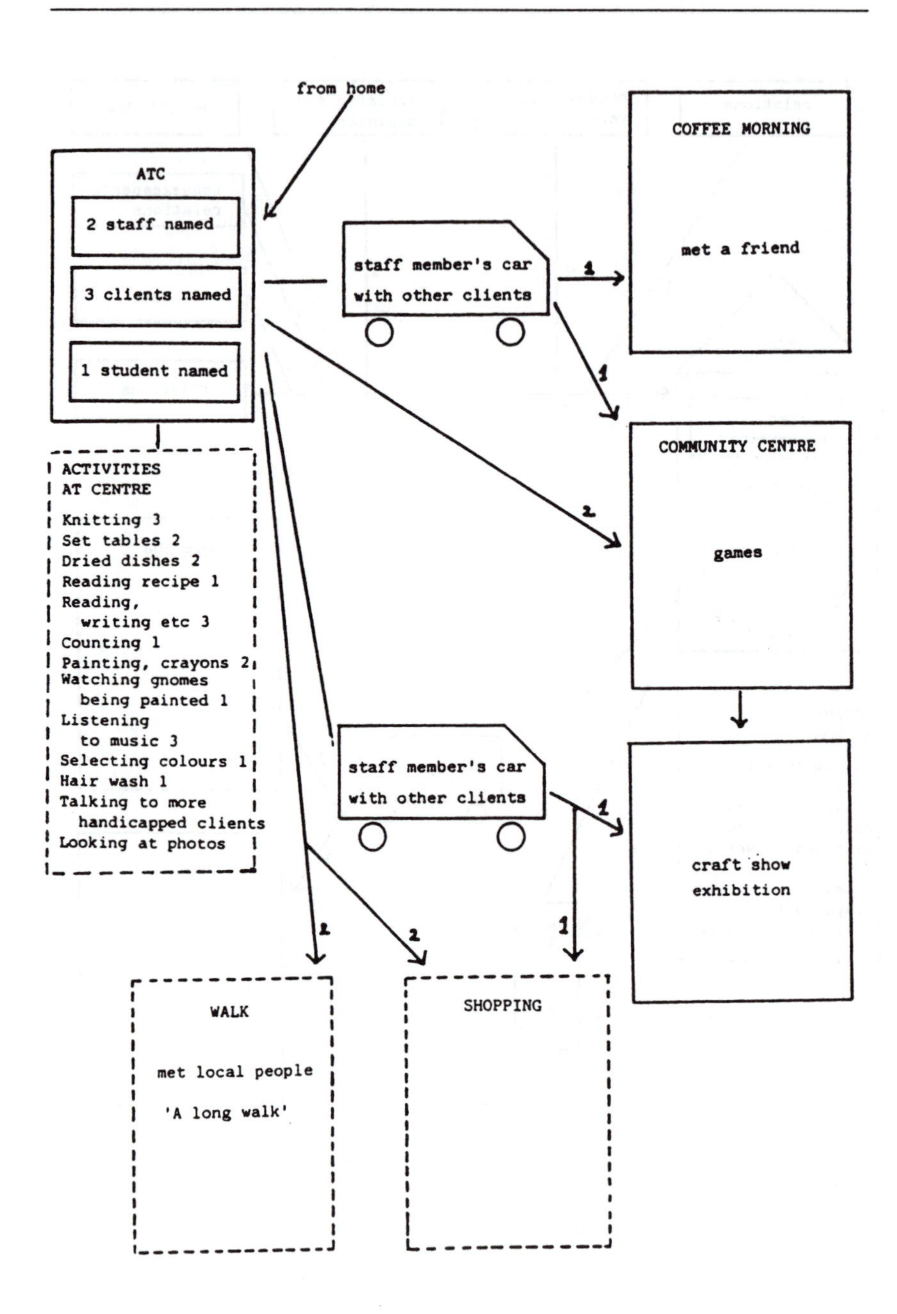

Figure 7.2 Anne – first monitored fortnight at the centre (1985)

Anne was for many years a patient in a day hospital for people with learning disabilities. For a short while, some years ago, when her mother died, she became an in-patient. But Anne was so distressed at this that her father moved house, on professional advice, to a place where a small local day service was available. Meanwhile, he employed a housekeeper who helps with looking after Anne at home.

The father's initial expectations of the centre were modest, namely that it would 'keep her happy'. During the research period in the 1980s, not only did Anne learn the things we have mentioned, but she was, as her father put it, 'happier than she had ever been in her life before'. Her experience at the centre is shown in Figure 7.2 for the first monitored fortnight. It was similar in the second fortnight, a year later (not shown) except that Anne now went out from home (accompanied), for example to church or to the shops.

1986

Anne has made great progress in learning specific tasks. During the past 18 months she had, for example, learnt to float on her back in the swimming pool, to brush her own teeth and many other little but important things.

Yet, as the following examples selected from the list of activities at the centre and staff objectives show, the emphasis of staff at the centre was less in terms of learning than on enabling Anne to enjoy life to the full. Learning was perhaps the product of this aim being fulfilled, rather than the starting point.

Activities and Objectives for Anne at her Day Service in 1986 (Second monitored fortnight)

Activities	*Objectives and Comments*
Listening to music	Enjoyment
Watching school sports	She likes to watch people doing things she cannot do herself
Watching more able clients	She enjoys it. She enjoys company. Opportunity to be in a smaller group which she likes

Activities	*Objectives and Comments*
Washing clothes	To help her to learn to do it for herself
Gardening	To follow through the fact that she volunteered
Hygiene	To get her to do as much as she can for herself
Outings	Enjoyment. Takes her out into the community
Games at community centre	To get her moving. She likes it
Reading	To help her from falling back at reading. She likes to read

Anne's father was getting older and less fit. The housekeeper was also elderly. What will happen to Anne in the long term ? Was the centre preparing Anne for the future? She was being given some domestic training and training in hygiene to help her to be more independent. Was this sufficient? The father (and probably the centre staff) would never see Anne as being able to manage without constant care. If this view is held, what does training for 'independence' mean?

A home help was introduced to help look after the father. This might have helped to postpone the time before decisions about Anne's future had to be taken. But Anne was likely to outlive her father and the kinds of questions we have raised must be faced. Should they have been faced sooner rather than later?

1988

After the research finished we learnt that Anne had begun a process of introduction to a hostel, so that she would be prepared for a possible future move from home.

1995

The proposed move did take place shortly afterwards. Progress continued at the day centre and at the hostel so that Anne was able to move again in 1991 to a smaller unit with three other people. At first she did very well, and her social network extended to include 'ordinary' activities in the community such as attending the women's guild and being active at church.

She continued to attend the same day centre for four days a week while on the fifth day she stayed at home to do her domestic work.

Meanwhile, the centre has adopted what was described as 'a radical new way of working'. For example, there is more emphasis on social education and employment preparation and less emphasis on crafts. Gone is the manufacture of garden gnomes! Instead, the centre has taken up desktop publishing.

These kinds of changes are perhaps too late to benefit Anne. Anne's support needs have, in fact, increased in the past four to five years in some respects after 'peaking' shortly after her move. She was described as having 'mentally regressed'. For example, she lost the ability to read a newspaper. Her memory began to deteriorate and she also appeared to be having some hallucinations. Though not yet medically diagnosed, she appears to be showing some early possible signs of dementia. It is planned that Anne will move to a new resource centre which will be in a position to respond more effectively to her changing needs.

JOE

1985

Joe was in his early 60s and his two sisters were considerably older. Both of the sisters suffered from chronic illness. Joe himself was said to be epileptic, but no fits were reported during the research.

Joe left school at 14 and worked for a few months at a fish processing factory. He then had other part-time jobs. After his father died, he lived with his brother and mother. When the brother married and the mother died he came to live with his two sisters. This illustrates a fairly common pattern. Adults with learning disabilities may move from one relation to another within an extended family. We have particularly found examples of this happening in our research in rural areas.

What is the role of the centre in Joe's situation? Joe says he attends because he likes it. His sisters' general view is that the centre keeps him busy, and that it is of benefit to them insofar as they are less worried. It will be noticed from the diagram for the first monitored fortnight (Figures 7.3 and 7.4) that Joe's activities

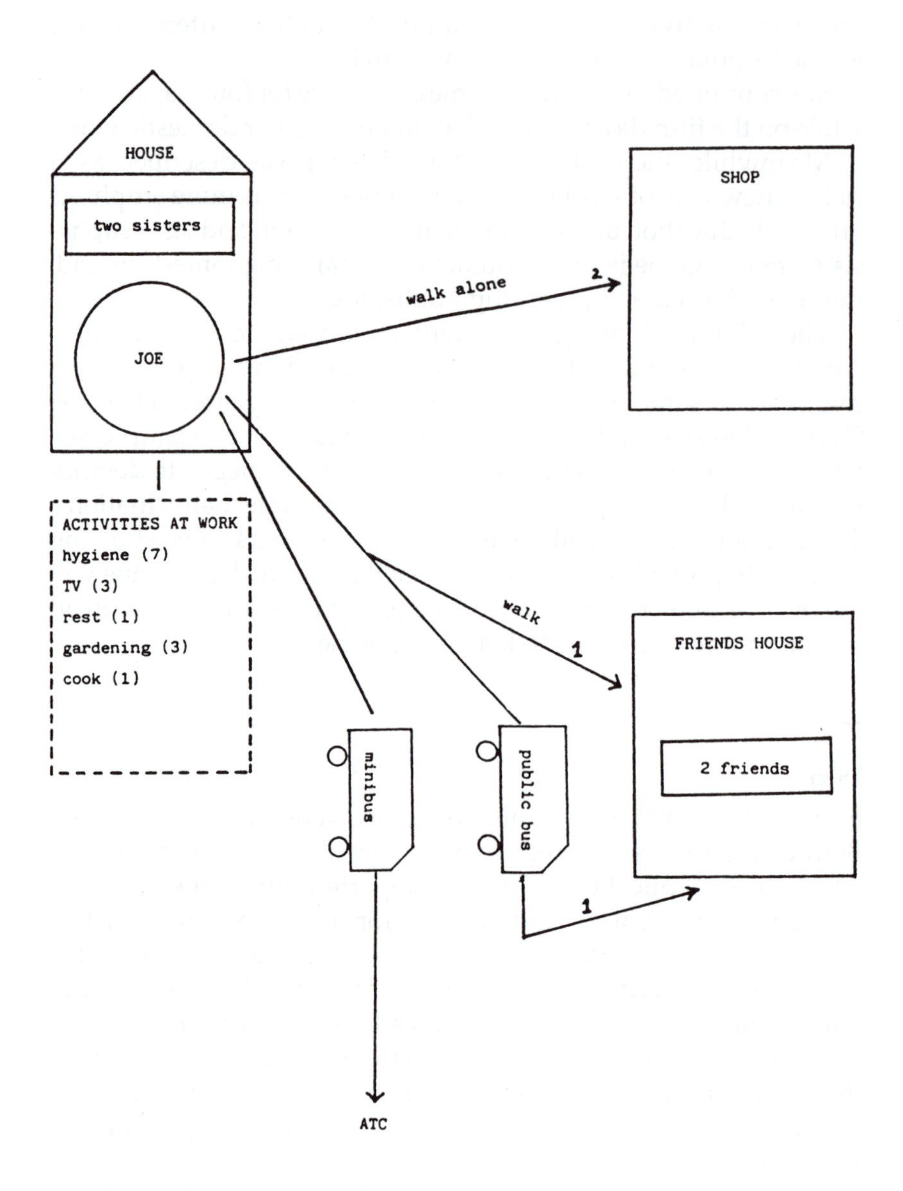

Figure 7.3 Joe – first monitored fortnight at home (1985)

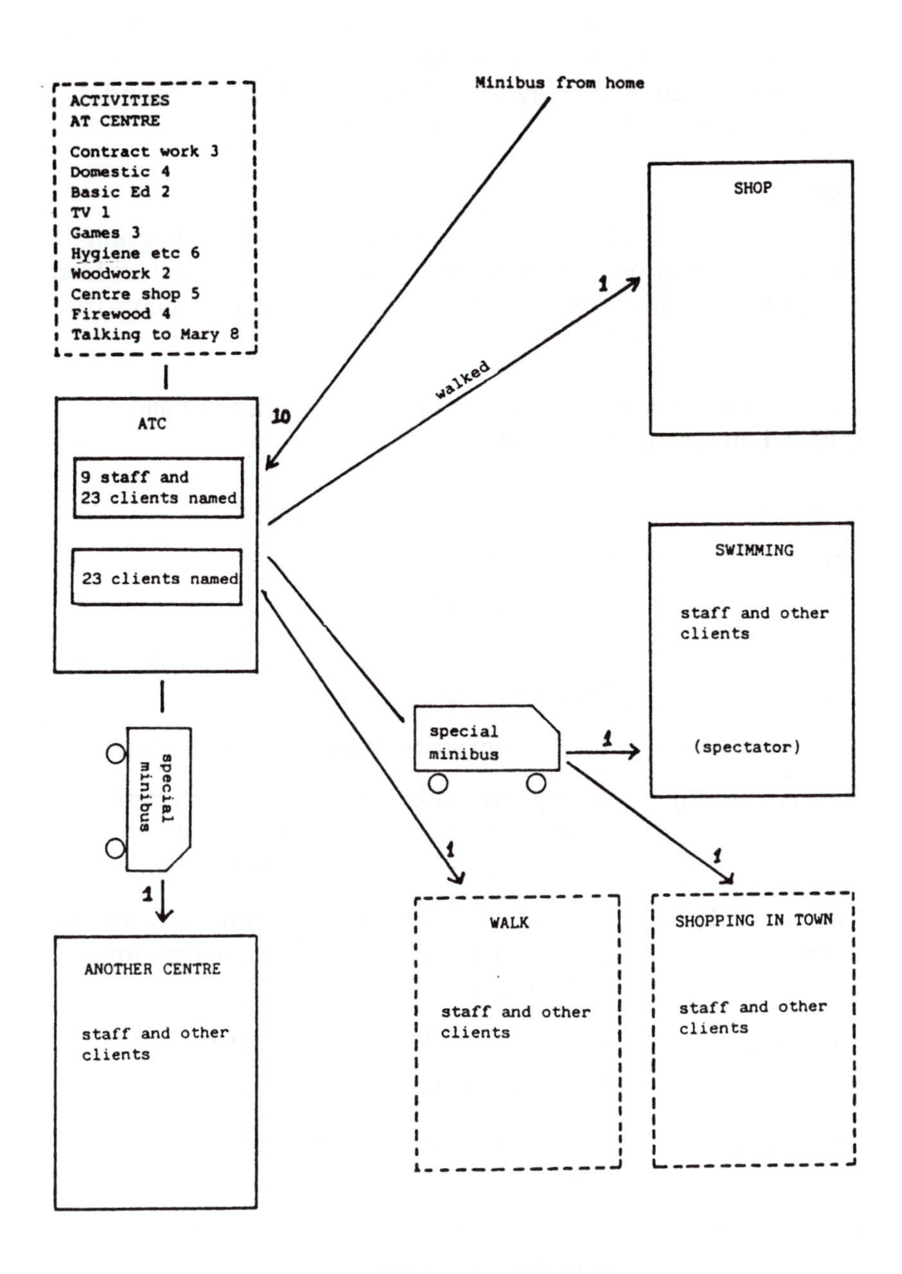

Figure 7.4 Joe – first monitored fortnight at the centre (1985)

range from contract work and woodwork to basic education and hygiene. Hygiene is particularly important so far as the sisters are concerned because, they say, Joe gets his bath at the centre and they are no longer able to give it to him at home.

1986

Joe did not keep full enough diaries for us to draw a diagram for the second monitored fortnight but we do have information from the centre list of activities and the objectives and comments from staff. These were as follows:

Activities and Objectives for Joe at his Day Service in 1986 (Second monitored fortnight)

Activities	*Objectives and Comments*
Art	Enjoyment
Craft	To improve skills
Woodwork	He enjoys it. To improve and extend skills. Maybe to help at home
Kitchen duties	To help him share chores with other clients
Kitchen training	To improve skills. To learn about appropriate equipment. (A problem is the lack of appropriate equipment.) To help at home
Visit to Garden Centre	Choosing and collecting equipment. To extend existing skills. (Problem of lack of time for such visits.)
Shopping	He enjoys it. Integration into the community
Disco	To be beside Mary (friend)
Sex education	To make him aware of different aspects of sexuality
Basic education	To improve basic skills. This is hardly necessary at his age.
Chopping wood	He enjoys it. Occupies him
Gardening	He enjoys it. Maybe it will help at home

DAILY STAFF DIARY REGARDING Joe COMPLETED BY Kerry DAY Wed.... DATE 17/4

	DURING THE MORNING	LUNCH	DURING THE AFTERNOON
LIST ACTIVITIES:	Was quiet as usual during Tutorial. Hygiene for 1st period. Mr Clark chopping sticks in garage		Had a shower and hair trim with Mr Williamson
STAFF EXPECTATIONS REGARDING EACH ACTIVITY	Good worker and helper		No problem. Needs a chiropodist
STAFF COMMENTS ON FULFILMENT OR NON-FULFIMENT OF EXPECTATIONS	Placid and consistent		Very helpful regarding other trainees. Fetches towels, soap and powder without having to be asked
OTHER COMMENTS CONCERNING CLIENT, e.g. BEHAVIOUR, ATTITUDE, MOOD	Good		No trouble at all

Figure 7.5 Joe – Staff diary page (1985)

Joe's programme had quite substantially changed since the first monitored fortnight, following a review at the centre. The sisters, however, were not consulted about these changes. When we interviewed them during the second monitored fortnight and asked for their opinion on each of the activities, they thought the gardening was excellent but, on the other hand, the exclusion of hygiene, and especially the bath or shower was 'deplorable'. His weekly baths had stopped, they said and his toenails needed cutting. They were too elderly to do these things for him.

The centre was giving more attention to Joe's social needs. Shopping was described as a means of integration into the community.

Joe had a girlfriend called Mary. The staff recognise the importance of this relationship and it will be seen from the list of activities and objectives for the second monitored fortnight that the comment beside 'Disco' was that Joe could 'be beside Mary'. He was also receiving sex education 'to make him aware of different aspects of sexuality'. However, there was no indication that Joe and Mary intended to live together.

What, then, was the future for Joe? When I raised this question with Joe's sisters, the reply was one of astonishment that such a question should be asked. They assumed that he would 'go on to help somebody else'.

Joe had spent 29 years attending an adult training centre. Was there an assumption that, perhaps at 65, he would leave? If so, why, and what would be the alternative? If not, what would be the continuing role of the centre in Joe's old age? In any case, was the programme of centre activities and staff objectives relevant to Joe's present and future needs?

1995

Joe 'retired' from the centre a few years later. More recently, one of his sisters at home died and the other sister moved with Joe to another area. For Joe, this meant a return to the locality of his childhood where other relatives lived, and where more support would be available from a third sister.

In spite of the greater distance, Joe maintains contact with his girlfriend.

POINTS FOR DISCUSSION

1. Would any of the following possibilities be appropriate in considering either Anne or Joe's long-term future?
   (a) To move to other members of the extended family.
   (b) To stay on in present house with support, taking on tenancy or ownership. (What support would be needed?)
   (c) Hospitalisation. In 1986, some parents or other carers liked to see this as a 'fall-back' possibility. This is not a realistic (or desirable) possibility today with the closure of long-stay hospitals.
   (d) Hostel or other residential or supported accommodation setting.
   (e) Support in 'ordinary' housing.
2. Joe was at home, intermittently working, until he was in his late 20s. At that time the adult training centre was newly opened and was looking for clients. Do you think any other alternatives could have been considered at the time? What, if any, alternatives would be available today?
3. What would be the continued role now, if any, of day services for Anne and for Joe?
4. What other services are needed in relation to any of the above possibilities?
5. Do you think the promotion of the client's happiness is a good starting point in considering centre staff objectives in these two cases?
6. In Joe's case how do you weigh up the advantages or possible disadvantages of what is perhaps a more focused programme in terms of preparation for independent living, with the carers' complaint about the lack of support to them when they stopped giving Joe a bath? (Staff comments on this activity while it was taking place are shown in Figure 7.5).
7. Some centres have 'carers' discussion groups'. What do you think of the idea? Is this best organised through the centre, or by an independent parents' group?

WHEN CARERS HAVE DIED

Anne and Joe had elderly carers. We now look at the situations of older clients with learning disabilities whose original carers had died.

Do adult training centres cater for people who are 'elderly'? Most centres do not and therefore the staff think in terms of clients 'retiring' at some stage? But, we may ask, retiring from what, and for what? What is their future?

In this set of three examples we apply these general questions more specifically to situations of people who, in fact, managed to live a long time in the community without day care. The question of day care arose only when their parents died.

WILLIAM

1985

William was in his early 60s. A few years before we first met him he was living with his brother, who was ill. William helped look after him. William was less and less able to cope and, apparently, he was locally regarded as an oddity, spending a lot of his time wandering about local streets and parks. Eventually he was admitted, as an emergency, to a home for the elderly, which catered for a total of 55 residents. Only after this was he introduced, for the first time in his life, to a day service.

The home and the centre were quite close together and William walked to the centre every day – although he said on wet days he could catch the bus.

Figure 7.6 gives us a picture of a fortnight in the life of William in the home for the elderly and attending the day centre for people with learning disabilities.

William was not in any way physically disabled. He was able to go out for a walk by himself to watch football. It was, therefore, in his case, superfluous for an orchestra and a church minister to visit him at 'home' although it might have been helpful for some of the other residents who could be physically incapacitated. The question may also be asked for someone of his age, who had not previously attended special facilities for those with learning disabilities, what 'learning disability' means? For the first 60 years of

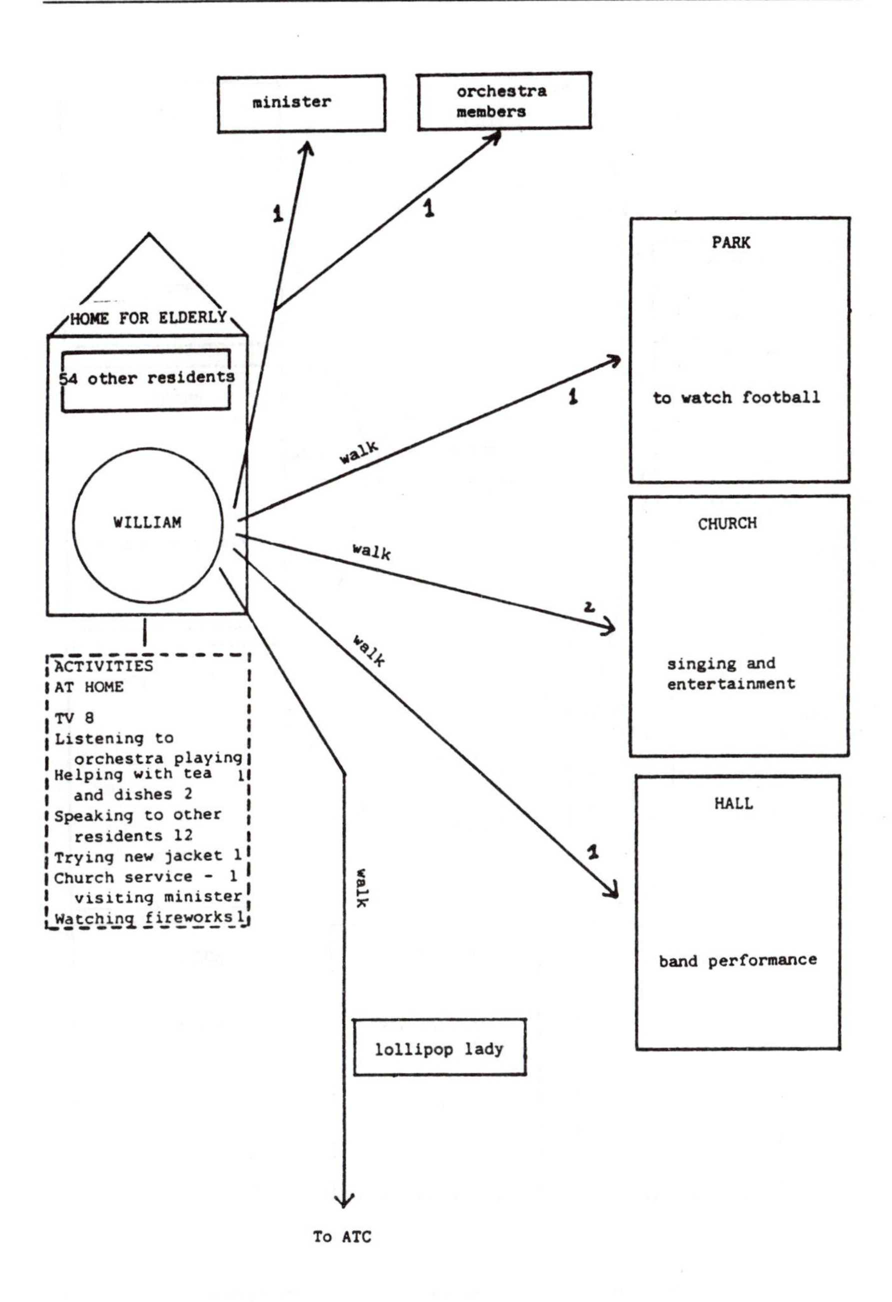

Figure 7.6 William – first monitored fortnight at home (1985)

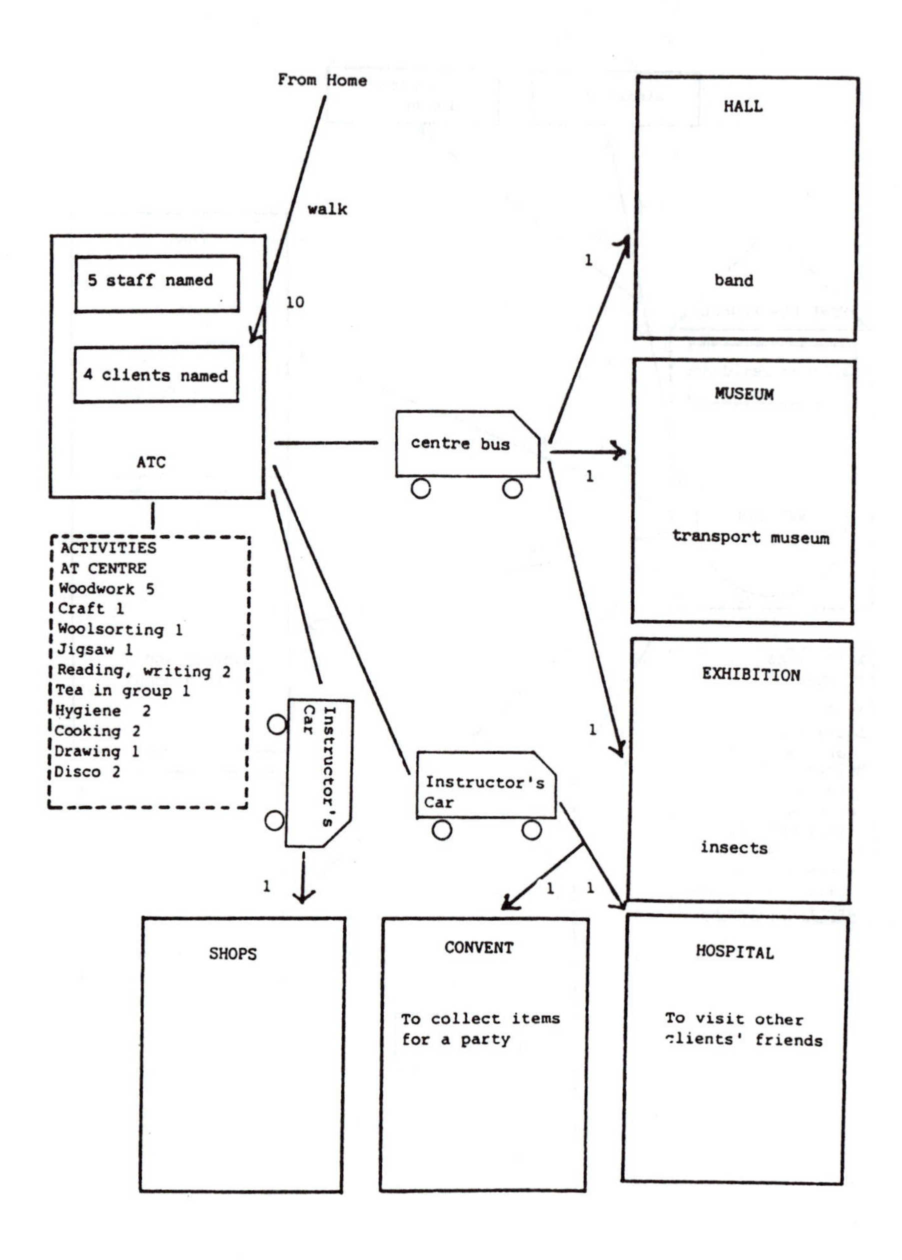

Figure 7.7 William – first monitored fortnight at the centre (1985)

his life he was probably not generally thought of as such. Why, then, should he suddenly be thought of as having a learning disability when he became older?

William could read and write a little. Staff at the centre claimed he did not understand the use of money. William himself said he could use the bus to get to the centre on wet days. Otherwise, as he wrote down for us, he walked to the centre everyday. He chatted to the lollipop lady *en route*.

Apart from the lollipop lady, William had no friends outside the institutional life of home and centre. If it is true, as is suspected, that he had no friends other than his brother before he was admitted to the home certainly he had not found any since. He had, however, made friends with other residents and other people with disabilities at the centre.

What was the centre aiming to do, and, in fact, doing for William? The network diagram (Figure 7.7) shows that first of all it was taking him out with other people with disabilities in special transport or the instructor's car. He visited an exhibition, a transport museum, a convent and also a hospital for people with learning disabilities where he met 'other clients' friends'. Once he went to the shops.

We looked in detail at what William was doing at the day centre and what the day centre staff were trying to do for him. We give below three separate accounts of a typical day during the first monitored fortnight. First, we have William's account – as recorded by a member of the staff at the home. Second, we have William's account as recorded by a member of staff at the centre for the same day and, finally, we have an account by members of staff speaking for themselves about their objectives for each activity undertaken during that day.

25 OCTOBER

1. William's account (recorded at the old people's home).

> Dressed, waited to see if rain went off. Spoke to my friends Harry and Tom. (After attending centre): hurried home in case I got wet. Nodded to someone who knows me. Ate supper, watched television and watched the orchestra in the House. Spoke to Jim (resident) and asked how he was keeping.

2. William's account (recorded by staff at centre):

   William said it was not far to walk. He would have taken a bus if it had been wet. He said he did not know the cost. He said he was on his own when walking. He walked past people. 'When I arrived, I took off my coat and had a seat. I had a cup of tea and then went to the education room. I did reading and writing.' He said he was a good writer. (After details of what happened at lunch-time): 'I was with Michael, big tall bloke, with red hair like a cowboy...' He had a bath and shave and felt refreshed. Then he said he felt sleepy and hungry. He said that in the education room, 'it is just like sitting in school. If I get too much money I get mixed up.' William reckons he did not go out on a trip today with the others because it was too wet. (At the end of being interviewed by the staff to complete the diary he asked if he had answered the questions 'quite good'. He said: 'You can't do any more than your best.')

3. Staff account of activities and objectives for William at the centre:

Activities	*Objectives and Comments*
Reading	William arrived late. He explained the story to me. Then he had a cup of tea in the group
Hygiene – brushing his teeth, having a bath and washing his hair	I hoped that William would learn to keep himself clean and tidy. The hygiene worked well. He does not brush his teeth thoroughly.
Crafts – he did a jigsaw and was working with wool	I hoped that with the wool he would be able to distinguish colours. The wool was a bit of a disaster. He could not distinguish most shades. He was in a very good and happy mood. His behaviour is never any problem

Between the two monitored fortnights I (researcher) visited William at the home for the elderly. I was told he was going to the centre later and later. This was because he liked to get his cup of tea at the home before he left. I was also told that his sister had died. It was reported that William helps another resident in the home to go through to breakfast and that he is friendly with others.

Meanwhile I had interviewed William himself. When I asked him why he went to the adult training centre he said, 'Because I was put there'. He added that it was to pass the time of day. He said, 'Time flies if you are working.' I asked him what he had learnt there and he said he had learnt to sandpaper and also to cook food. But he added 'I could cook before. My brother and I used to take turns about.' His favourite activity, he told me, at the centre was cooking. He said, 'I get to take cakes home.' He said he would like to go to the centre more often rather than less often and at weekends too but for parties, not work. He would like more parties and dances at the centre.

1986

The following is a summary of the activities undertaken, and comments from staff, during the second monitored fortnight:

Activities	*Objectives and Staff Comments*
Domestic	Enjoyment. He tends to take over, seeming to know it all, e.g. peeling potatoes and using the washing machine
Hygiene: had a bath and shave	Eventually hope he'll be able to do it himself without prompting. He tends to come in unshaven. He enjoys being told to shave. A problem is lack of space for this activity and the group is too large for the room
Outings	For enjoyment and seeing other people
Disco	Mixing. He tends to be a loner

Activities	*Objectives and Staff Comments*
Reading and writing	No real aim because of his age and ability. He enjoys education and he is strong in this area. He is of an age where he is not going to change. He has everything catered for him at home
Workshop: constructing little kits – sanding and varnishing	To give him something to do and keep him interested. He can do these things. But he builds them all wrong and you try to tell him how to do it but usually you have to do it for him. It is cramped as a workshop, used for putting things out. It gets cluttered up
Horse riding lesson	Company – rather than being on his own. He wouldn't go on a horse. I don't know if there's many people that would take the time to talk to him
Helping to organise layout for dance	Just something for him to do
Various errands in connection with the place of another evening dance	Something for him to do (in activity)
Visit to swimming baths	Enjoys spectating – asks to go swimming. Enjoys cup of tea
Educational outing in minibus. (Visited park and then another adult training centre)	Something to do. He tends to get isolated a lot. He arrives very late so that it's hard to get him started in the group. He wants the toilet as soon as he goes anywhere. His age means there's not a lot we can do with him educationally

Activities	*Objectives and Staff Comments*
Outing to swimming baths because of gala being held the next day	Enjoyment as spectator. To get him out. This is the only group he will willingly take part in
Final staff comment: 'William won't go into any group at all. I spoke to the manager about this and was told as long as he is just getting a break, not to push him.'	

After the second monitored fortnight I discussed with William's key worker at the home what were the important places and people in his life. The important places were a church hall, local shows and watching football in the park. Important people were the lollipop lady and staff at the home. The lollipop lady was just important to him as a friend rather than offering any kind of help. He chats to her on 'dry days'.

1995

We heard that William had died a few years ago.

POINTS FOR DISCUSSION

1. William was in an old people's home with 54 other residents. Is this the most appropriate setting? What alternatives could there be?
2. Is there any evidence of the effects of institutionalisation on William?
3. Should William have been at a day centre for adults with learning disabilities What would have been the alternatives? Should William have gone to a centre earlier in his life?
4. Granted that William was attending an adult training centre, what would you suggest as an individualised plan which is more constructive than simply finding him 'something to do'?

5. Comment on the choice and relevance of each of the activities and objectives listed.
6. Do you accept that for someone of William's age (in 1985), it was too late to learn? William did seem to be making friends. How do you evaluate the possibilities for using these friendships as a basis for enabling William to lead a more independent life?

JENNY

1985

Jenny was about ten years younger than William. When we first knew her she lived as a lodger with her sister, brother-in-law and their children. The sister explained that Jenny liked to be independent, keeping herself to herself. She said they used to be more involved in trying to keep Jenny clean, but they had not had to do this since Jenny had been taught hygiene at the day centre. Before coming to the centre, relatively late in her life, Jenny (like William) had wandered in the streets.

Jenny's abilities were somewhat similar to William's. She could prepare a simple meal, use public transport, undertake simple domestic chores. She was less able than William in expressing herself. According to her sister, Jenny tends to panic when, for example, she gets a letter from the benefits agency.

Jenny led a restricted social life, doing only necessary shopping on the way back home from the centre. She had no friends outside the centre.

1986

Between the first and second monitored fortnights, Jenny's brother-in-law died. For a few weeks after this she seemed to slide back into a more slovenly personal appearance. But by the time of the second monitoring she had recovered and was taking part in a greater variety of centre activities. It may be, also, that the centre staff were becoming more aware of her needs. It seems they now had a concerted plan to prepare Jenny to be more independent as she became older. Below is a summary of the activities and staff objectives and comments for the second monitored fortnight.

Activities	*Objectives and Comments*
Hygiene: Washing her clothing	To teach her to do it for herself. General learning. To take her out to the launderette.
Hairwashing	To teach her to do it on her own in a handbasin. (She can already do it in a shower at the centre, but she does not have a shower at home)
Sewing: care and repairing of clothes	To be able to sew a button and sew for herself
Basic education: reading and writing. Social sight vocabulary, (e.g. signs)	
Shopping	To improve and reinforce shopping skills. To learn correct use of money
Games	To motivate her. Otherwise she tends to sit and draw
Cookery	To improve cooking skills. To improve her knowledge of cookery, including being able to compare prices of items
Musical movement with exercises	To increase her co-ordination
Sports	To help her join in with others in a team. She tends to stand out from the crowd
Music and singing	Stimulant. Relaxing. She is inclined to curl into herself. Withdrawn.

While much was done to improve her 'survival' skills at the centre, little attention appeared to be paid to her lack of social life outside the centre. Yet the question must arise, did Jenny want her social life enriched? Once I asked her if she had any particular friends and she replied: 'No, I keep myself to myself.' Yet she was not without interest in other people and places. She was fond of knitting.

Although this did not feature as an activity in the list of centre activities, she could often be found during the lunch break knitting squares for Ethiopian refugees. She also told me she had enjoyed a recent centre holiday because they were 'out all the time'.

1995

Jenny is now aged 64. She moved from her sister's house in 1990 to a residential home run by a voluntary society in the same town. She still attends the same day centre where there is no fixed policy about 'retirement'. She can continue to attend after she is aged 65. When she does leave, the manager of the home told me they would arrange a programme of day activities including attendance at old people's clubs. She was already attending one such lunchclub from the day centre.

It seemed that Jenny had become a more sociable person since her move. She goes out with a small group of the other residents shopping, to a café and to clubs. She attends a further education college for an evening arts and crafts class with another resident, who also attends the same day service. She has one particular (female) friend in the home.

Jenny continues to be in close contact with her sister, staying with her alternate weekends.

I was told her self-care had improved. Personal cleanliness was not now a problem. She does some of her washing. She remained keen on art and knitting. She was described as more talkative and 'more settled'.

The home where Jenny lives was converted some years ago from a children's home and some of the staff had returned to work with a new client group. The ages of the current residents ranged from 26 to over 65, with the majority in their early 30s. When I visited, the staff and residents were preparing for a holiday in chalets at *Butlins*.

POINTS FOR DISCUSSION

1. Is it desirable to involve Jenny in activities with other people in the community, and not just within the centre? If so, how would you set about doing this?

2. Many centres recognise a 'retirement' age for their clients (perhaps 60 or 65). Yet, it could be argued, as Jenny becomes older she will need more, not less, support. Would you consider some other form of organised day care for people who are elderly, or is the proposed programme of activities organised by a residential home (1995) a better idea?
3. Do you think Jenny's programme of activities at the centre would help to prevent an otherwise likely admission to a home for the elderly? Was the outcome for Jenny at a residential home with a mixed age-group the best? What would be the arguments for and against this in preference to preparing Jenny to live in a small flat perhaps with her friend? What kind of support in a flat would she need and who would provide it?
4. What advantages has Jenny had that William did not have?
5. Would William have benefited from the kind of centre programme Jenny had (perhaps earlier in his life)?

JESSIE

1985

Jessie was nearly 60. Like William and Jenny, it was only in the latter part of her life that she came to attend a day centre. Unlike William and Jenny, however, she was, from a very young age, known to have a learning disability.

Jessie's sister also has a learning disability, as does her sister's daughter (Jessie's niece) with whom she lived. All three attended the same residential special school. When they left school the two sisters were at first supported by their parents and when their parents died members of the extended family helped. A neighbour of the family had been, and still was, also involved in giving support. The niece was regarded by the researcher as the main support person at home – though in different ways they helped each other.

The day centre Jessie attended was an unusual one. It grew out of a club which Jessie and her niece attended. It is different from the traditional idea of an 'adult training centre' in two main respects. First, part-time attendance is normal and in this instance

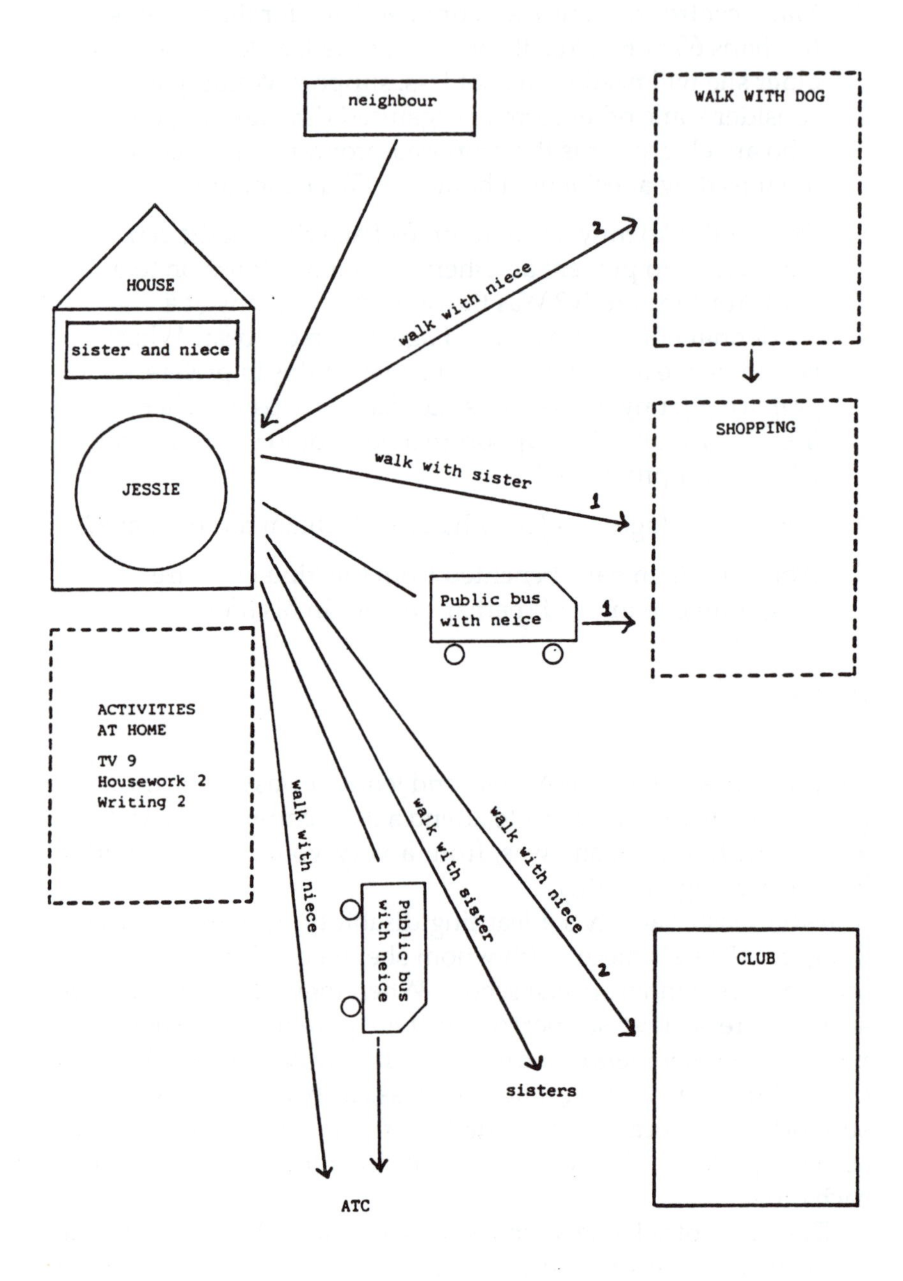

Figure 7.8 Jessie – first monitored fortnight at the centre (1985)

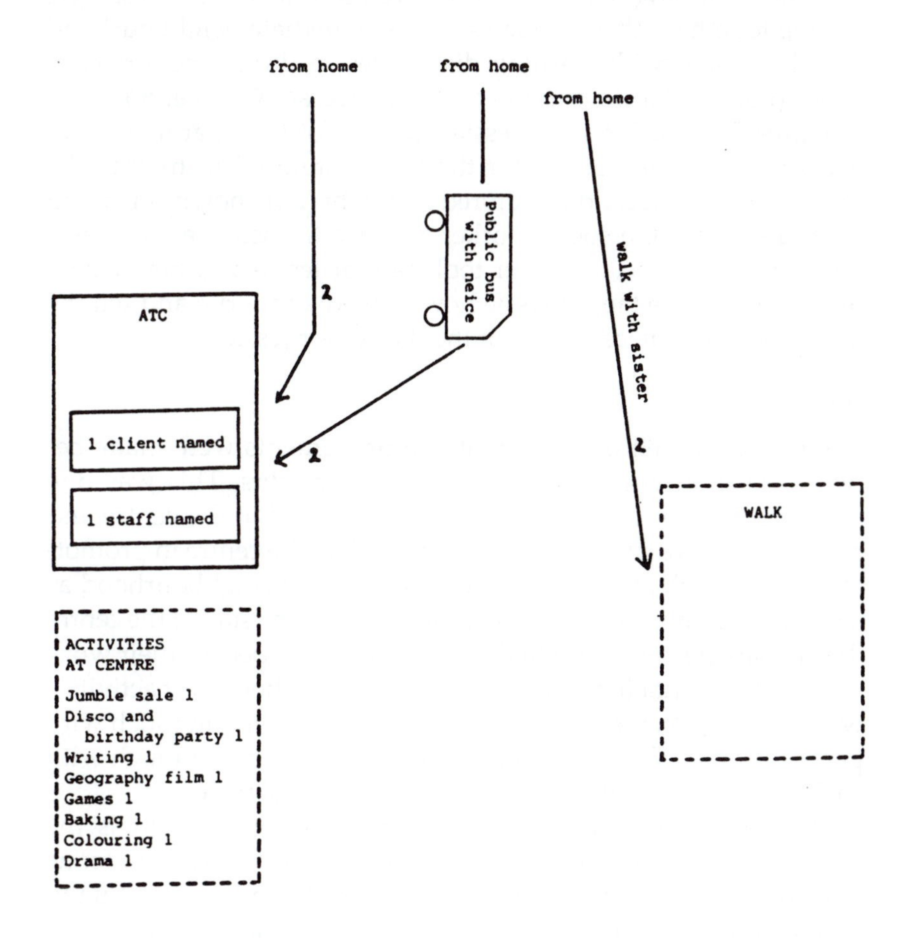

Figure 7.9 Jessie – first monitored fortnight at the home (1985)

Jessie and her niece attended on different days. Jessie particularly enjoyed coming on a day which is set aside for an afternoon club. She also attended on another day when there was more emphasis on social learning. Second, the centre set out to be a resource, linking together other resources in the immediate neighbourhood to help people with learning disabilities in direct and practical ways. (For a fuller description of this centre, see Chapter 8.)

Figure 7.8 and 7.9 show Jessie's pattern of living at home and her activities at the centre for the first monitored fortnight. The diagram for the second monitored fortnight (not shown) included visits also from the social worker and health visitor as well as a neighbour. The social worker took care of Jessie and her sister's money. The niece taught Jessie how to read and write and tell the time. It was the niece who kept the diaries for Jessie.

1986

The researcher felt quite dramatic improvements were made between the first and second monitored fortnights. This was due partly to the stimulation and activities received at the centre and partly, and more subtly, to the part played by the centre in promoting the network of support at home and in the neighbourhood as a whole. Perhaps the recording undertaken by the staff at the centre did not always do justice to this 'community' aspect of their work because it was not in terms of 'instruction' or other direct activities with clients at the centre. It was in terms of keeping in touch with people, using informal opportunities to put people in touch with each other and maintaining contact with other services.

What does come across in the comments of the staff is the importance of the social function a centre can perform for someone like Jessie. For example, Jessie, during the first monitored fortnight, had to perform at her birthday party. She was, said the staff, 'very happy and enjoyed singing a song in front of the group. She always enjoyed a party and if asked would get up and sing with absolutely no embarrassment. We made a video of her singing and she was overjoyed to see it played back to her.' There was, however, an educational side to the centre activities. The purpose of baking was 'being able to measure and mix well'. By the time of the second monitored fortnight the educational tasks were more sophisticated.

She baked a few small cakes, and she was said to be 'very good at this'. An educational morning was spent 'learning to listen' in relation to writing.

The object was to try to get Jessie to write clearer and learn addresses without needing to copy. It was reported, however, that she was 'still copying only'. Some of the activities, with an educational purpose, were informal and spontaneous. For example, she was 'tidying up her geography folder' in order 'to encourage awareness of the world outside'.

The centre manager's comment on Jessie's support needs was that she 'accomplishes something new every day and is growing in confidence all the time'. The researcher added:

> This too is my impression and I feel the centre works particularly positively for Jessie in this respect. It is perhaps ironic that I am saying this for a woman nearly 60 years old, rather than for the younger clients. After leaving school Jessie was at home from 1940 to 1981 and I wonder how many other Jessies there are unknown to the authorities, who could perhaps benefit from a similar service, albeit at a younger stage in their lives.

The neighbour who offered practical and social support was not in any way related but she had known the family for many years in an area where neighbourliness still counted.

1995

The home situation was sustained until, a few years ago, the niece died and the sister, who developed a physical disability, moved house. Jessie, then in her late 60s was admitted to a home (for the elderly) where she is now happy and doing well – still enjoying singing in front of groups.

POINTS FOR DISCUSSION

1. Does centre practice in this case differ from the routines of the more traditional day centre you would expect? Would Jessie have benefited from the centres attended by William and Jenny (so far as we can tell from the examples given)? Would

there have been any differences in the way you would have approached William's situation, or Jenny's situation, had you been the manager or a staff person at Jessie's centre?

2. This is an instance of people with disabilities supporting each other in the context of support they are receiving from outside. The family unit continued to function after the death of the parents. Do you think this is a good idea? What would be the alternatives?
3. What do you think of the combination of social and educational activities as the main thrust of a centre programme for Jessie?
4. What would you suggest is the role of the field social worker in this case?
5. What is meant by a resource centre? Do you think this function is fulfilled in this case?

CHAPTER EIGHT

A Part-Time Day Service

INTRODUCTION

There is some evidence that people with learning disabilities who have left home and are living on their own in ordinary housing, as distinct from being in residential accommodation or part of supported housing schemes, are sometimes denied access to day services. Once they have left their parents' home, the motive of respite for providing day services is removed. Some day services, however, are aware of this issue and have especially attracted single or married people who, without support, would be vulnerable and in some cases homeless. One such centre is 'Brookside'.

BROOKSIDE

Brookside – the fictitious name we will give to this centre – is situated about a mile from the centre of a large city. It is in an area of extensive redevelopment.

Brookside has only had part-time attenders since it started in the early 1980s. Originally the part-time attendance was to ration places. Brookside shares an old school building with various other projects including a senior citizen's project and some community education activities.

Brookside's manager had previous experience as a field social worker. She turned the setting to advantage. Those attending the centre became a resource to others. Help was given to the elderly. Soon help was being given to others, e.g. help in running a playgroup.

Part-time attendance came to be seen to be the best means of ensuring that learning at the centre was transferred to other settings. This was particularly relevant in preparing people with learning disabilities to live independently in the community.

JIMMY

1984

Jimmy attended a special school. He recalls: 'School was horrible. We got no education. They just told you to shut up all the time.'

His parents died when he was fairly young and he went to live with his sister. But she became ill, had to go into hospital and later died. For the next 20 years Jimmy lived in hostels or wandered about. As he told his own story:

> I had a lovely home which I shared with my sister. But when she went into hospital I smashed up the house. I was drinking heavily. For the next 14 years my sister was in hospital and I continued to drink. I stayed in various lodging houses and skippered. Then one day I decided I had to pull myself together and now I rarely take a drink.

His Roman Catholic religion was a source of strength and apart from attending church regularly he became a helper at a church club for homeless people which he still attends and which we have fictitiously called the Wayfarers' Club (see Figure 8.1). Through the Wayfarers' Club he came also to help at the senior citizens' project within the same building as Brookside Day Centre. The staff there felt that he would benefit from the part-time services of Brookside Centre along the corridor. He had been attending for a few months when he first became known to the researcher responsible for evaluating Brookside, Fiona Harkess. She described Jimmy in her notes at the time:

> Jimmy lives on his own and is in his late 40s. He could be described as a quiet survivor who uses the help of professional services appropriately but whose lifestyle is probably some distance away from that of the general population. Having been homeless for a number of years, he maintains his contacts with the homeless scene, through attending almost daily an evening club for homeless men. He sees himself as a helper at the club and this role is important to him but I

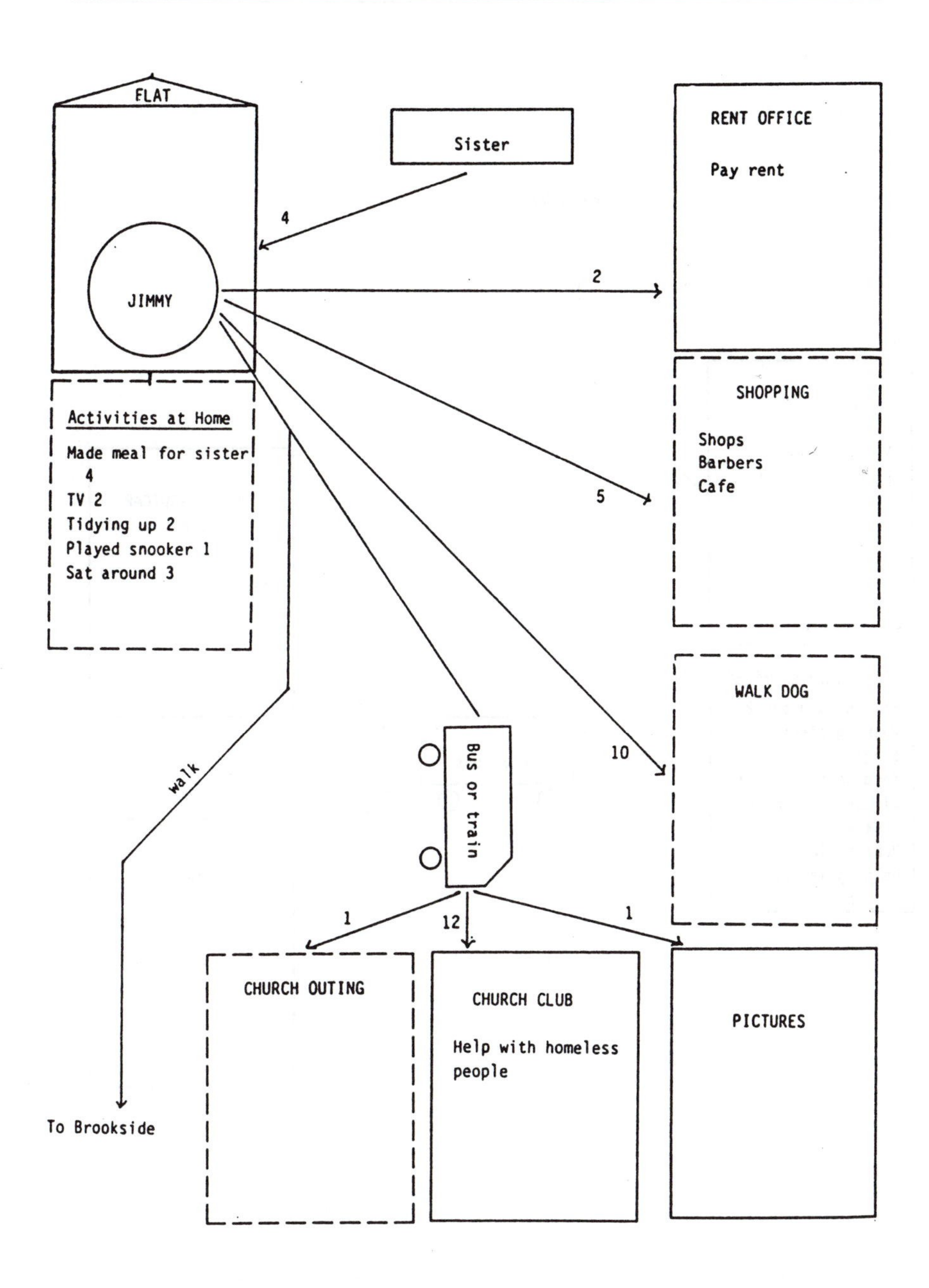

Figure 8.1 Jimmy – first monitored fortnight at home (1984)

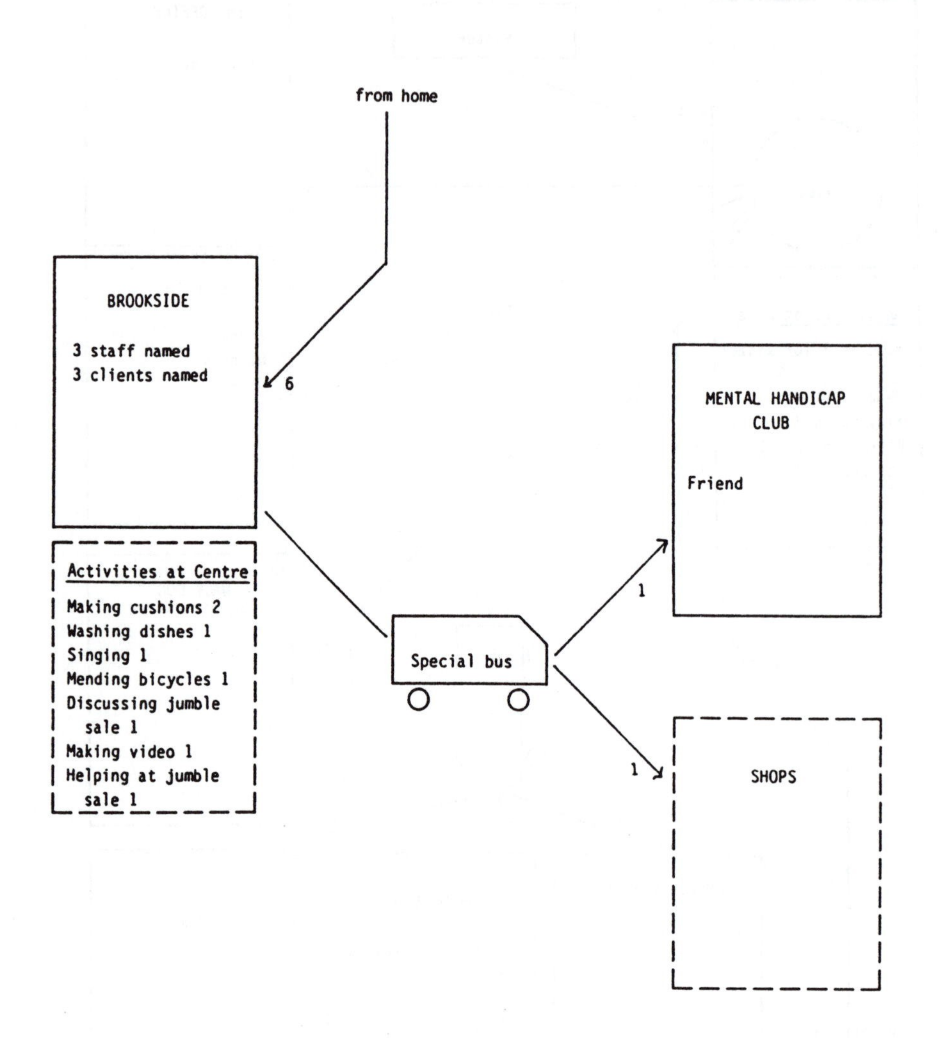

Figure 8.2 Jimmy – first monitored fortnight at the centre (1984)

> would suggest he probably has more in common with the users of the service than with the traditional perceptions of volunteers...
>
> Despite his somewhat unkempt appearance, the many layers of clothing necessary to the long-term homeless, Jimmy has an air of dignity as he sucks at his pipe and gives his definite views on how to deal with housing officials and the department of social security.

Jimmy himself felt very positively about Brookside. Amongst other comments he said:

> I really like the centre. There's nothing wrong with it. It keeps me out of the house – I get bored stiff in the house. I learnt about helping people (e.g. in the senior citizens' project). You get to feel better yourself when you are helping people. I have learnt handicraft and I would like more. I could help teach people this. Centres shouldn't be like school. People shouldn't be bossed around. There's nobody bossed at our centre.

Jimmy attended initially for two days a week and this was subsequently increased to three days – the third day being to attend a social club. Jimmy was described by the staff as a sociable person but the club gave him the opportunity to make specific friends.

The staff recognised that Jimmy needed help in managing in a settled home of his own. The explicit aim from the staff was to help him to live more independently. At the same time the centre was sensitive to the part that the church club played in his life and because part-time attendance was taken for granted there was no question of his having to give up attendance at the club, or any of his other activities such as art work at home, in order to attend the centre. Figure 8.2 shows how his attendance at the centre relates to his other activities. It will be seen that he is now in touch with another sister.

The centre recognises his need to be a helper to others and to make a valid contribution from his own life experience.

Sometimes Jimmy went to the centre explicitly to help others. For example:

> At Brookside jumble sale: helped behind the counter. He did a good job, sold a lot of trousers. Helped people to find right sizes in shirts and trousers. (Staff comment on Jimmy's diary.)

But the educational side was also important. When Jimmy first came to the centre his reading ability was extremely limited and he needed help with forms. Although he had a flat of his own he wanted to move to a better one and this, with help from the centre, he eventually accomplished. An instructor visited him at home on the days when he did not attend. (This does not occur during the first monitored fortnight which in some ways was not typical as there was an emphasis on social activities with a lead up to Christmas.) Jimmy also needed help in managing money and with cooking. At the same time his interest in craft was encouraged and here he was both learning himself and helping others. In his own words: 'I would like more craft work. I could help teach them this...(though) I go to the centre to learn this.' At the same time the staff could say: 'Jimmy's learning all the time'.

1986

Figure 8.3 and 8.4 show a fortnight in Jimmy's life in March 1986. He had now moved to a different flat which was a lot further from the centre. He had to travel by two buses to get there. He was now back to attending two days a week. On one of the days he went out from the centre to buy food for lunch and made an onion omelette with soup and sweet. In the afternoon of the same day he was with a small group learning to play whist. On the other day of the week he had craft work and was learning bead art. In the afternoon he went out for a bowling match. On one of the days in the following week he was sorting through a geography folder.

It will be seen from Figure 8.3 that Jimmy's network was somewhat enlarged compared to the earlier fortnight. He was still in regular contact with his sister – Jimmy was concerned about her health. He had reason to worry in view of the ill health of his parents and of his other sister who died after a long period in hospital. His sister, together with a cousin, was temporarily staying with him. A richer 'structure for living' is beginning to form.

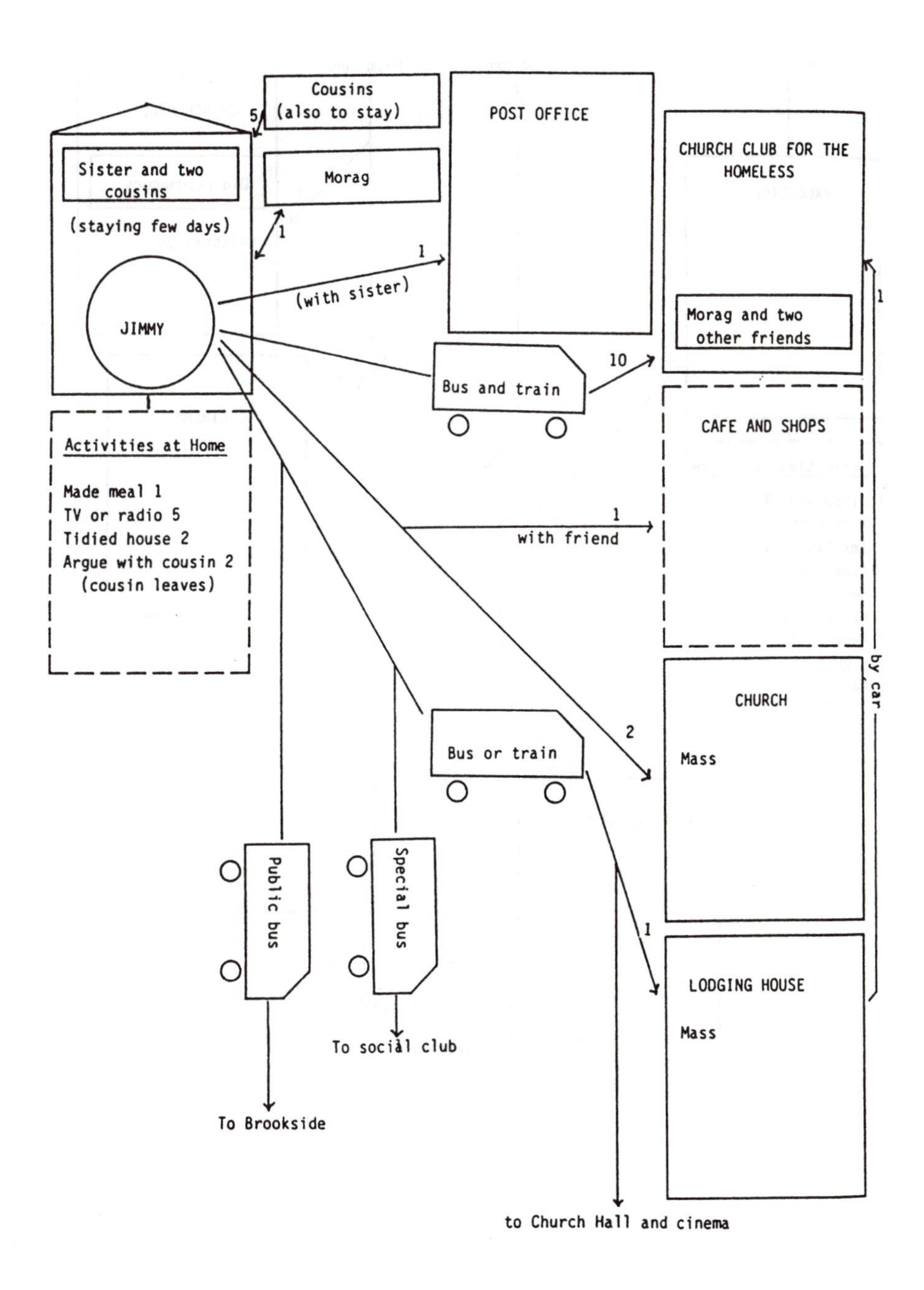

Figure 8.3 Jimmy – second monitored fortnight at home (1986)

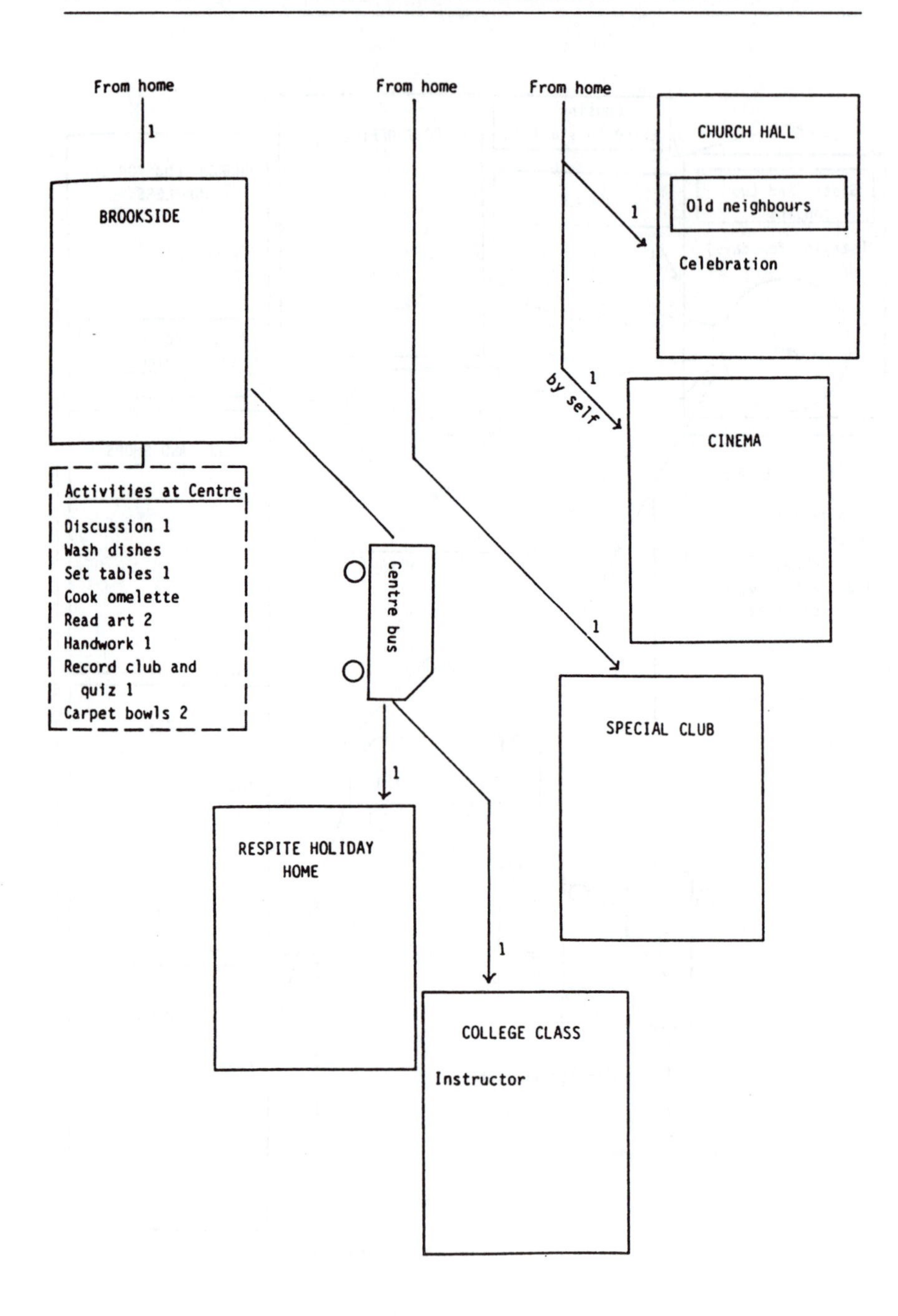

Figure 8.4 Jimmy – second monitored fortnight at the centre (1986)

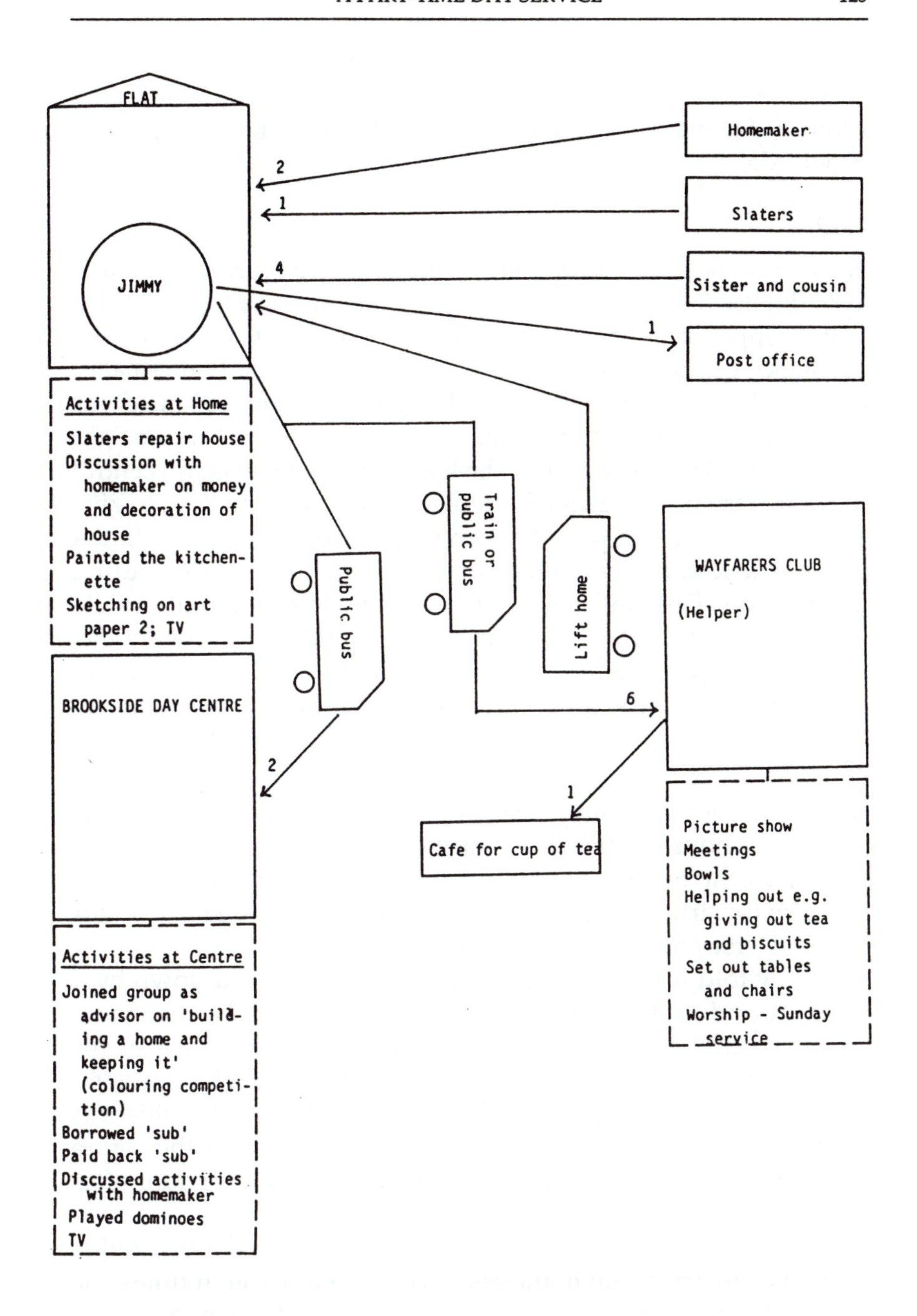

Figure 8.5 Jimmy an additional monitored week (1988)

It will be noticed that Jimmy was also attending a course at a further education college. This was for basic education. He also attended Monday Special Club for baking, which was arranged through Brookside.

1988

Next, we look at a week in Jimmy's life over two years later in June 1988. Figure 8.5 is for a week in this case and not a fortnight. He only dropped into Brookside once a week and instead he had the assistance of a home-maker in his own house. The home-maker discussed decorating with him and at the same time the house was being repaired. She brought him paint one day and he straight away painted the kitchenette. The Wayfarers' Club was still central to his pattern of living and at Brookside he continued both to give and receive help. He joined a group as an adviser on 'building a home and keeping it' which was also a theme for a colouring competition. This was making use of Jimmy's artistic skills while at the same time he was also involved in building his own home. His activities with the home-maker were discussed at Brookside where practical help as well as recreation continued to be offered.

1995

Jimmy is now attending Brookside three days a week. He has moved to a house owned by a housing association, not far from the centre, and he receives ten hours staff support each week. When I met him (by arrangement at the centre) he was dressed in a smart suit and jersey and was clean shaven.

Jimmy told me that last year he had been knocked down by a minibus and had spent some weeks in hospital. He had now recovered and though he walked slowly, partly because of his continued arthritis, he was in general good health. There was no sign, at first, of the former pipe Fiona had referred to, but this was because there was nowadays a no smoking policy in the centre rooms and later I saw him smoking in a seat in the corridor after lunch.

In the past few years Jimmy has had his ups and downs, and at one stage he was again homeless. 'I've had a few rough times,' he said, 'all behind me.' But he acknowledged with a smile: 'Sometimes you do things.'

Jimmy gave me an idea of his weekly routine: Wednesdays he attended the Legion of Mary where he said he was a leader. He has also recently been on holiday with the Legion of Mary for five days. Most weekends he stays with his sister.

Jimmy told me his cousin had died last year. He still has a brother abroad (in New Zealand) but there is no contact.

Jimmy told me his weekly routine:

Mondays:	'Nothing'. Watch television. 'Sometimes good programmes and sometimes not.'
Tuesdays:	At Brookside. He said he did handicrafts but said 'I'm not very good at making'.
Wednesdays:	Meeting at the Legion of Honour. Home help comes.
Thursdays:	Brookside.
Fridays:	Brookside. Home help comes.
Weekends:	Goes to stay with his sister.

Jimmy said Brookside had been 'very useful – a good help'. He said he liked coming to talk to the men and women.

POINTS FOR DISCUSSION

1. Consider the variety of needs that Jimmy has and how the centre has helped to meet them during the past ten years.
2. In what ways does Jimmy's situation illustrate the various aspects of learning to live independently?
3. Compare, for Jimmy, the significance of Brookside Day Centre in comparison with the Wayfarers' Club. Are they complementary?
4. Do you think it would be helpful, or unhelpful, if Jimmy attended Brookside Day Centre fulltime? Why?
5. Consider the importance of Jimmy's own motivation in this case and in what ways does the centre facilitate this?
6. In what ways does part-time attendance facilitate the transferring of learning from the centre to the home situation?

7. Can you understand Jimmy's anxieties about the health of his sister in view of his earlier life history? Could more have been done to help him with these feelings and if so, by whom?
8. Discuss the problems of maintaining service continuity when someone moves house. What might have been the consequences of a change in home carer for Jimmy when he moved to a new house in a different area?
9. What further plans would you want to discuss with Jimmy?

FRED

1984

Fred was slightly older than Jimmy – he was in his early 50s when the researcher, Fiona Harkess, first made contact in 1984. Fred, like Jimmy, had attended a special school and he recalled: 'I liked school. I'd like to go back to school. But the teacher didn't bother with me at all. I used to be reading the same page over and over again. I didn't get to learn any more.'

We do not know a great deal about Fred's early history. His parents had died and his only brother lived abroad. During his early adult life he had several jobs. He was a message boy when he was aged 15. He was employed in the steelworks and in a furniture factory and in shops. He also worked in a plant nursery. Gardening has remained a particular interest. Then he worked on a farm in the country. He recalled:

> My social worker came up to the farm and asked me if I wanted to go on holiday. She told me that I didn't have to go back to the farm. They only paid me a pound a week and they would only let me go to the pictures and back, not to go to the pub or anything. So when I left for a holiday I told the social worker that I didn't want to go back to the farm and so she got me into a hostel (in the city).

When he was in his late 40s, Fred married. His wife attended an adult training centre full-time. Fred had a temporary job as a washer-up in a hotel. When the job came to an end Fred asked his social worker if he could be referred to Brookside. Fiona Harkess recorded:

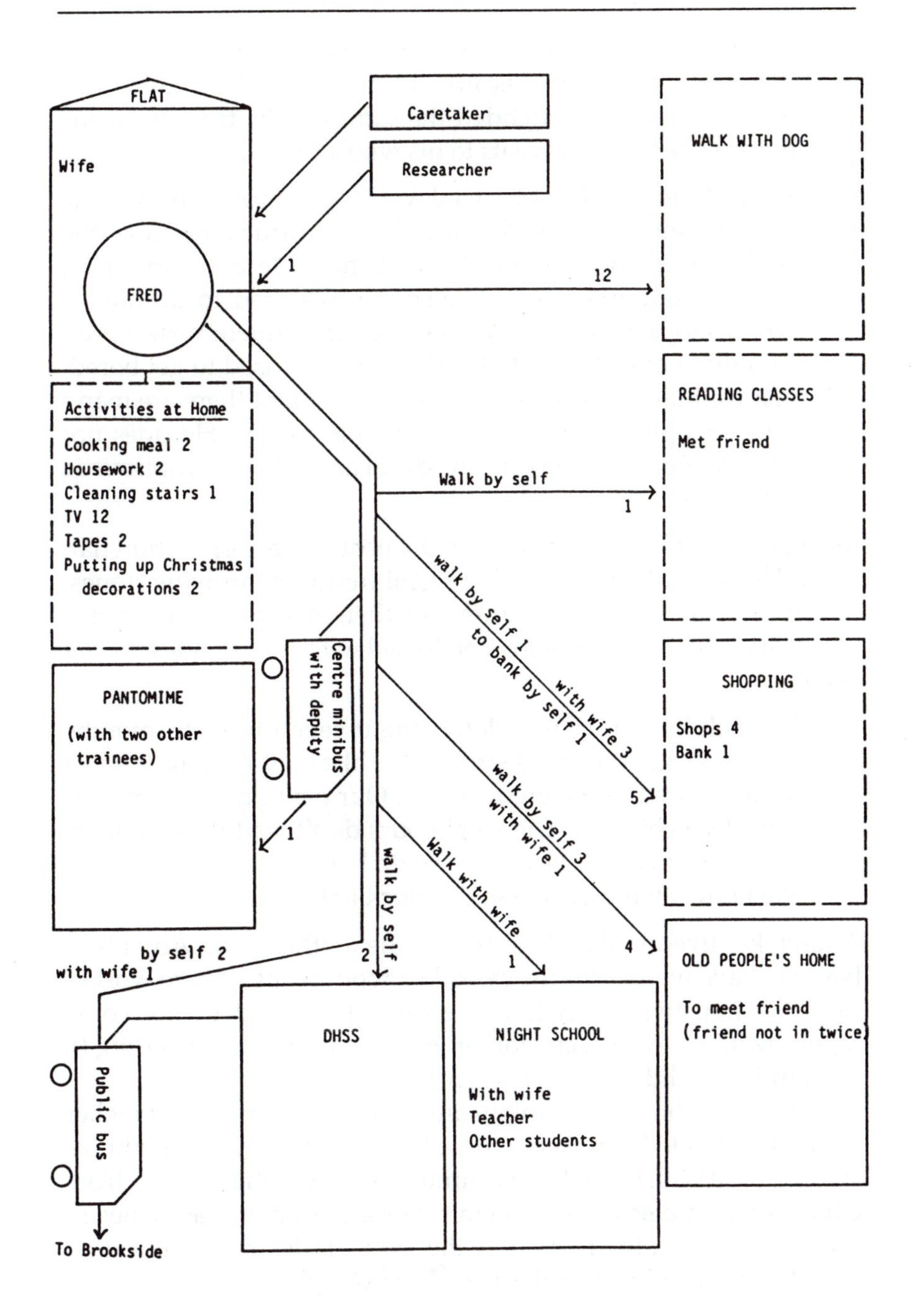

Figure 8.6 Fred – first monitored fortnight (1984)

> The arrangement was made that he attended Brookside rather than his wife's centre because it was assumed that they may argue a lot if they attended the same centre, from previous experience of Fred's visits to his wife's centre.
>
> Fred attends the Centre two days a week, though he says he would prefer to attend three days. It struck me that the part-time attendance enables both his wife and himself to have outside interests, but also releases Fred to do housework, shopping and taking the dog for frequent walks. Fred said that before he started at the centre he used to get bored, just walking the streets. I would suggest that there are many other people like Fred, not attending centres. He does not present himself as very disabled and has a cheerful, optimistic view of life.

Meanwhile, Fred had moved from the hostel to a corporation flat. He and his wife did not like it there. Children kept throwing stones. So the staff at his wife's centre put their names down with a voluntary housing association concerned with people with special needs.

> We didn't have to wait long, about seven to eight months before we got this (present) flat. We like it. Not all the tenants go to centres. Some are working. Our next door neighbours have two children. The neighbours don't visit us – we keep ourselves to ourselves – but we do have a chat on the stairs. We know all the people in the block to talk to.

A caretaker lived in the block and, as the mother said, 'Any problems we have we can see the caretaker about them.' A care worker from the housing association used to visit 'but does not come regularly now'. The social worker was also available, according to the family but did not visit regularly.

Figure 8.6 shows a fortnight in Fred's life during November 1984. He attended Brookside three times during the fortnight including once with his wife for a jumble sale. Activities ranged from education and discussions to craft work, drama and activities in preparation for Christmas. But the staff diaries show that each activity had an educational aspect. For example:

Tuesday 20 November 1984

Activities	*Staff expectations and comments*
Welcome to centre	Immediately to make the day's programme known
Morning tea and daily discussion regarding today's programme	The day's programme is made known to all trainees and is an opportunity to discuss any anxieties arising from the programme. Trainee's personal problems are discussed privately on a one-to-one basis
Education – distinguishing various objects by their colour and shape, e.g. traffic lights, pillar box, zebra crossing etc.	
Shopping – exercise of buying a record for another trainee's birthday	To improve speech, confidence and freedom of choice
Lunch with other trainees and staff	Social activity and related skills
Games hour – pool and darts	Finger movement – dexterity and ability to compete
Attended birthday party for another trainee	Learning opportunity for socialisation
Took part in video film – taped during birthday party	Confidence building

Other activities during the same week included watching the film *The Sound of Music*, potting plants and repairing bicycles. They also rehearsed *Hansel and Gretel*.

Much of the work of the centre in this case is done outside. Centre staff visited Fred regularly in his own home and it will be seen from the network drawing that the deputy manager went out with them shopping and to the pantomime theatre. Also, outside the centre, Fred attends reading classes and night school. He has contact with a particular friend in an old people's home. He takes responsibility for his own visits to the bank and to the department of social security. The programme could be summarised as helping Fred to sustain and develop his married life. The researcher commented:

> The majority of Fred's activities tend to be organisation-based, that is night school trips out with the centre etc. However, this was not a diary where I felt everything was in the world of mental handicap. The special housing that Fred lives in also accommodates people who do not have learning disabilities as good neighbours.

1986

Figure 8.7 shows the network diagram for the second monitored fortnight in March 1986. Fred now attended an adult literacy class with his wife. He went out shopping with his wife as well as to the bank and the family was friendly with another trainee from his wife's centre. Meanwhile at Brookside Centre, Fred had been introduced to voluntary work with the senior citizen's project in the same building. He helped in preparing tea there. He was now attending Brookside four days a week. The following are the statements of staff activities, objectives and comments:

Activities	*Objectives and Comments*
Attended craft class at further education college (two sessions)	To accept criticism from lecturer. To improve the quality of his work as a result of accepting criticism. Interaction with other students
Working with elderly in senior citizen's club including serving luncheons	For benefit of his marriage – to give him an extra day out of the house (in view of some domestic problems with his wife). Self-esteem
Prepared Formica topped tables and repaired chairs	Likes to be busy and likes the status of having made something. This again is related to his domestic situation. It gives him esteem at

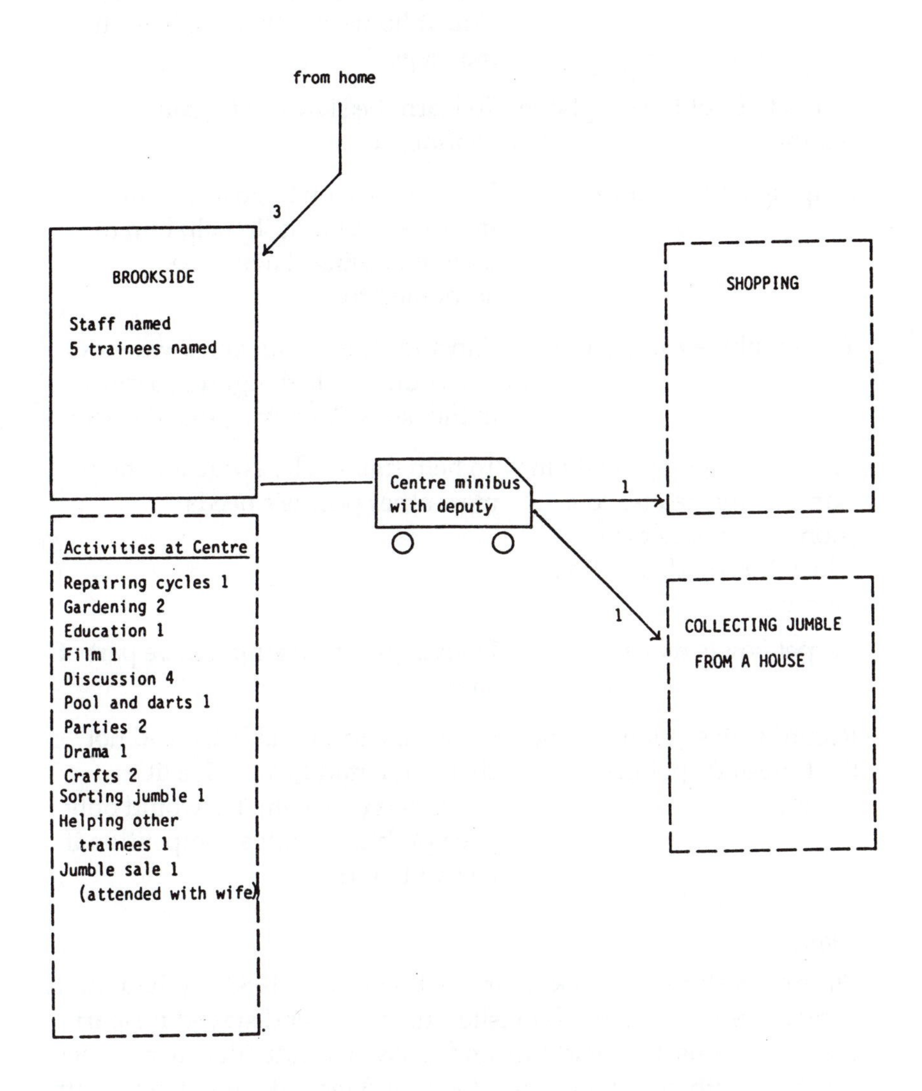

Figure 8.7 Fred – second monitored fortnight (1986)

	home if he can carry out the same skill at home and this will help the marriage
Correct use of the telephone session	To learn the skill and to gain confidence
Helping with inventory	Having a set job to do and to do it. To improve counting. To help him to learn that things have to be accounted for
Geography – America	Fun and stimulation and awareness of a country which figures so much in the news. An awareness of vastness
Prepared letter to a child in Gambia (this relates to a sponsorship scheme in which Brookside Centre is involved)	To help trainees be aware and help meet other people's needs
Carpet bowls match	Enjoyment and learning to be part of a team
Record club session – name the time and spot the celebrity	Being able to sit and listen and not chat in the middle of it. He likes being part of a team. He would only have problems with a competition if he had to write

1988

Figure 8.8 shows a week in Fred's life in June 1988. He had made contact with a cousin who visited his home and stayed for part of the week. His life was full and busy. He attended a tenement meeting with other tenants. His attendance at Brookside Centre had now reduced to once a week where he attended for a drop-in club. He had support from a key worker attached to the housing association. He had a particular mate called Sam but he also went shopping with his wife and cousin. We are told that until recently he was working on a community programme and it will be seen

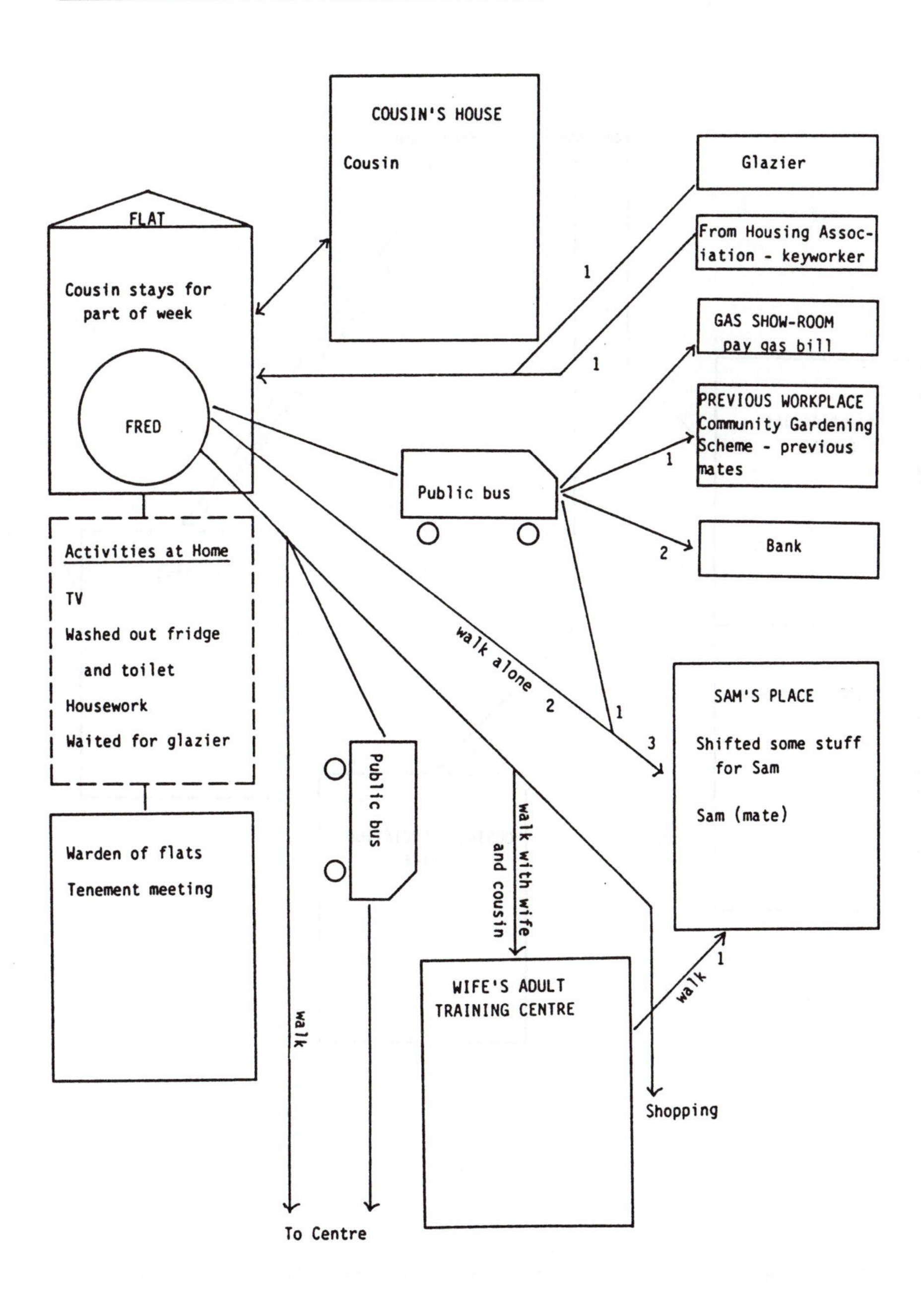

Figure 8.8 Fred – an additional monitored week (1988)

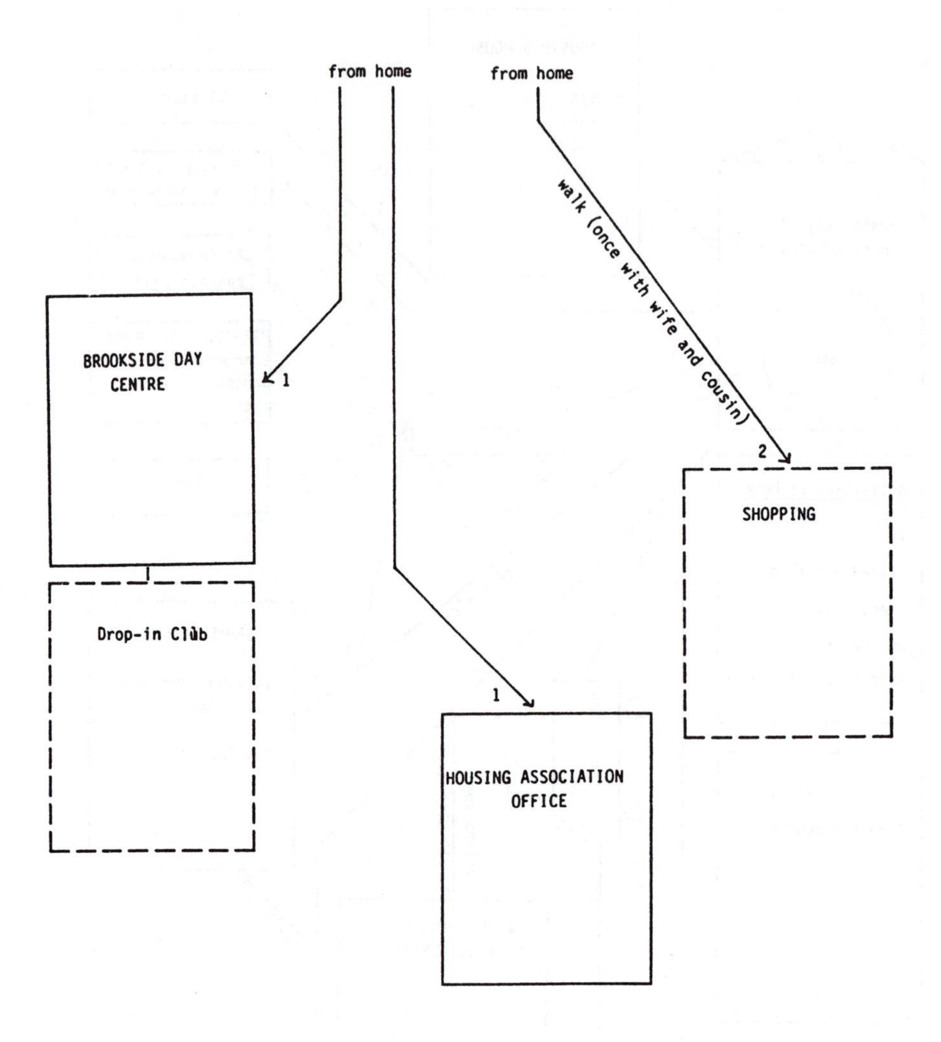

Figure 8.8 Fred – an additional monitored week (1988) (continued)

that he returned to the project to meet his previous work mates. A footnote to the diary told us that Fred was shortly going to attend an interview for employment.

1995

Fred no longer attends Brookside but he called in specially to see me (Philip Seed), whom he had not met but knew to be a friend of Fiona Harkness. He knew I had come to see him to update this book.

His wife no longer attends a day centre but stays at home where, for the time being, someone Fred described as his 'half-cousin' stays with them. Recently, all three of them went to *Butlins* together with his cousin's boyfriend and her 8-year-old daughter. He said his cousin would shortly be moving out to get married but she had assured him that he could visit often.

Fred told me of his weekly routine:

Monday:	Housework.
Tuesday:	Night school. He also, he said, goes out on Tuesdays to 'buy sweeties.' He added he was 'very busy on Tuesdays'.
Wednesday:	'Sometimes out and sometimes not, depending on the weather.' I was told he has speech therapy on Wednesdays. Home help comes.
Thursday:	He said he often goes out with his cousin.
Friday:	Home help comes.

Fred had recently had a social work review, which had resulted in the speech therapy. (I found him a little difficult to understand and he has a slight stammer.)

Fred told me he had not worked since we had last been in touch. He still saw some of his work mates from the past.

When I talked to Brookside's manager, she reflected that it was good that Fred no longer needed to attend a day centre, though, she said, he was not living 'independently' if that meant he could do all the things himself normally expected of being a tenant.

Of Brookside, Fred said, 'They help people. They've helped me.'

POINTS FOR DISCUSSION

1. In what ways, if at all, has attendance at Brookside helped to improve Fred's quality of life over the 11-year period covered?
2. What are some of the particular problems when adults with learning disabilities marry? Discuss the support that this family received and in particular the role played by Brookside Day Centre in sustaining the family as a unit. (The material is incomplete insofar as the research was not concerned with what was happening at the day centre attended by Fred's wife.)
3. What issues particularly arise for people, whether they have learning disabilities or not, who marry late in life? Is there evidence that Brookside Centre was aware of these issues and dealt with them sensitively?
4. How would you set about developing a richer social network in this case? Answer this with relevance to the original absence of relatives from the network and in relation to the fact that, as the researcher says, many of the contacts are 'organisation-based'.
5. Fred has been employed in the past. Did the social worker do him a service or a disservice in, apparently, encouraging him to leave his job on the farm?
6. It could be argued that Fred's full-time job had been helping to look after his wife. Consider the implications of this for the proposition that, with improved employment prospects, Fred could be able to find work.
7. What does training for independence mean for someone who has mild learning disabilities, in his early 50s and married to another adult with a learning disability?

ANDY

1984

Andy was aged 34 when Fiona Harkess (researcher) first visited him in the autumn of 1984. At that time he lived with his elderly parents in a council flat in a three storey building on a main road.

Andy had two brothers, one of whom in 1984 was a long-stay patient at a hospital for people with learning disabilities. Andy himself went to a junior occupation centre. He spent several periods away from home. He suffered from epileptic fits and was once in hospital for 16 months after a violent incident. He came home again at his parents' request. After another incident he was again temporarily admitted to hospital but again returned home. In current terminology he might be described as having 'challenging behaviour'. One particular problem was that he enjoyed drinking and alcohol does not mix with the drugs he was taking to control his epilepsy. He was prescribed pills for a week. Sometimes he took too many and then took none during the last days of the week. This made drinking easier but it could also induce more fits.

In November 1984 when his position at home with his parents was becoming increasingly difficult, he was suspended from the centre and only attended a jumble sale during the monitored fortnight. The researcher, Fiona Harkess, commented:

> During the research study period (1984–5) Andy tried to slash his wrists on more than one occasion and was also violent in the centre. His problems perhaps stem from a difficult background. On my visits to the home I have noticed a tension in the air... Dad's gangrene and resulting amputation of one of his legs are adding to the upheaval in the home just now... The mother has mentioned that Andy's drinking at home is a problem.

Although Andy was suspended from Brookside Centre, the centre staff were, with the social work department, intensely engaged with the family in trying to devise a suitable structure for living for Andy in the future. Fiona Harkess recorded:

> Social work staff, both at the centre and at senior management, felt that a hostel placement or a group home placement would be too difficult for the other residents. The most feasible solution seems to be a flat on his own, possibly remaining in the parental home when mum and dad move. I feel that if this occurs the centre will continue to be very important for Andy, providing him with a stable contact. My impression is that the centre provides stability, reality, friendship and acceptance in Andy's life. Andy himself says that he finds it a lot easier to talk and mix with people in the centre than he would

> outside. Andy's needs are not easily slotted into the learning disability day centre category in that I see his problems as coping mainly with a psychiatric rather than a learning disability problem. Brookside seems to cope with this to a certain extent and it is questionable how far a mainstream centre, less geared to individual need, would be able to do so.

The researcher went on in her notes to comment that a strength at Brookside was their greater use of counselling rather than an authoritarian attitude towards people who transgress centre rules of accepted patterns of behaviour.

1985

By August 1985, Andy was attending Brookside three days a week and a new activity was horse riding. Six trainees were accompanied by two teachers and 'a considerable number of volunteers'. The researcher recorded:

> Andy struck me as much more settled and more in touch with other people in the centre, than previously. For example, he was much more ready to talk to me and he told me that he was trying hard because he didn't want to be banned from Brookside. He liked the place. The manager told me his drugs problem had stopped, that is they have managed to control his excessive taking of his epileptic drugs. Problems at home continue. Andy told me his father was very depressed at the thought that more of his leg might have to be removed because of the spreading gangrene. Andy's brother was, at that time, decorating the house.

1986

Another monitored fortnight took place in March 1986. Andy now had a place in a lodging house. He had a particular friend there and he engaged in some of the activities of the house. He visited his parents' house every other day. He only went once during the fortnight to the pub. Brookside Centre was particularly important to Andy at this stage. Though still excluded from attending the centre on certain days this was compensated for by the fact that he attended on other days. The following is a statement of the activities and objectives at this time:

Activity	*Objectives and Comments*
To include him in a group	Helping with bowling where he will be less of a problem. To get through to him that he is not the only one with problems. This is not achieved. He doesn't really help – he is not compassionate. He has to be pushed to act as a volunteer all the time. He sees it as a way of staying on at the centre so that he can be allowed back on Wednesdays and Fridays
Writing session	Arrived late. Missed writing session and did exercises
Set tables for lunch	To take part in centre activities
Telephone session	Element of fun – e.g. to find the cricket score. He is proficient. Also to help him learn how to deal with agencies like the DSS
Counting dishes for inventory	Responsibility – to have a set job and to do it
Discussion with manager and deputy	A chance to examine his future
Had chat with other trainees attending drop-in club	

1988

There was another monitored week over two years later. The parents had moved into sheltered housing and Andy had been given the tenancy of a flat. It was within walking distance of his parents. Figure 8.9 shows his pattern of living for a week in June 1988. He had assistance at home from a home support and day care worker. This was a scheme to employ local people to befriend and help a socially isolated person like Andy. He met Andy in the evenings. He had taken him to visit various clubs and during a particular week illustrated in the diagram it will be seen that he

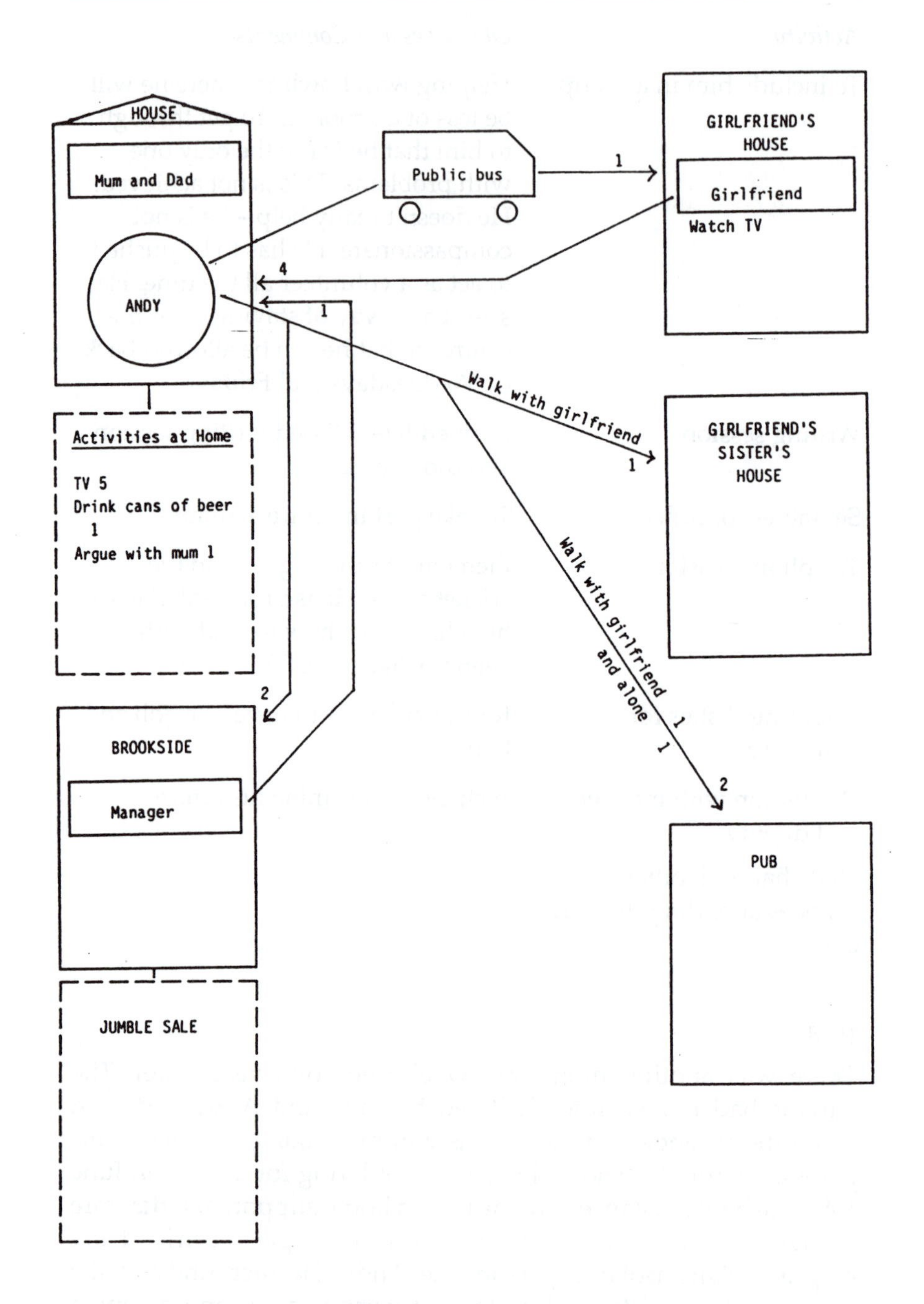

Figure 8.9 Andy – a monitored week (1988)

accompanied Andy on two occasions to visit his parents' house. Andy spent a great deal of time with his parents. On two occasions Andy visited the bar by himself where, he said, he was friendly with one of the waitresses. On one occasion, his diary recorded: 'Stayed in mother's till 9 pm went to the bar for a few drinks – not drunk – went home 1 am. Talked to pub staff. Tried to cadge money – no chance.' Earlier in the day he had 'words with dad'.

Andy was at this time attending Brookside regularly two days a week. Amongst other activities, he attended the same teach-in discussion on 'building and keeping a home' attended by Jimmy. Jimmy, in fact, was mentioned as someone particularly important for him at the centre. Helping others at the centre was a welcome role for Jimmy and accepted by Andy. Meanwhile, Andy brought his weekly washing to the centre where he used the washing machine, operating it himself.

1955

In 1995 we enquired what had become of Andy and heard, sadly, that he had died.

POINTS FOR DISCUSSION

1. What issues does Andy's situation raise about 'challenging behaviour' of people with learning disabilities attending day centres? Discuss the use of exclusion as a sanction together with continued individual programme planning while he is excluded.
2. To what extent does Andy's behaviour reflect his wish to leave home and yet his dependence on his parents for support?
3. With hindsight, can it be said that Andy should have left home earlier in his life? If so, how could this be accomplished and what sort of help should be offered in training for independence?
4. Comment on the role of the home support worker.
5. Do you consider that Andy has a drink problem? If so, how can this be tackled? What are the particular problems of drink for people with epilepsy?

CHAPTER NINE

The Challenge of Being Able-Bodied with a Severe Learning Disability

TIM

1985

Tim was aged 27 when the research started. He was fit and physically capable. He had a severe mental handicap but there was no specific medical condition associated with this. Furthermore, Tim looked, at first sight, to be a very 'normal' person. He was not very tall nor very short nor very fat. Seen in the swimming pool, he would be indistinguishable from 'normal' people.

One would perhaps go further and say he was unusually fit. He loved outdoor activities. He looked young for his age, and this appearance was reinforced in situations where he was treated more like a child than an adult.

Tim could be considered an example of a case of 'challenging behaviour' at the centre at the time the research started. Why was this so? Because he was fit and strong it was hard physically to control him. He needed more attention than others, but the attention was, at first, directed to attempts to contain and control him. However, the centre was undergoing a period of rapid development during the research and we are able to study the progress that Tim began to make in response to this.

Tim and his family lived in an urban community where many families would be described as 'close-knit'. Tim's family was an exception. In another respect, however, the family was typical of other families with a son or daughter with learning disabilities. Tim was the only 'child' remaining at home after his brothers and sisters

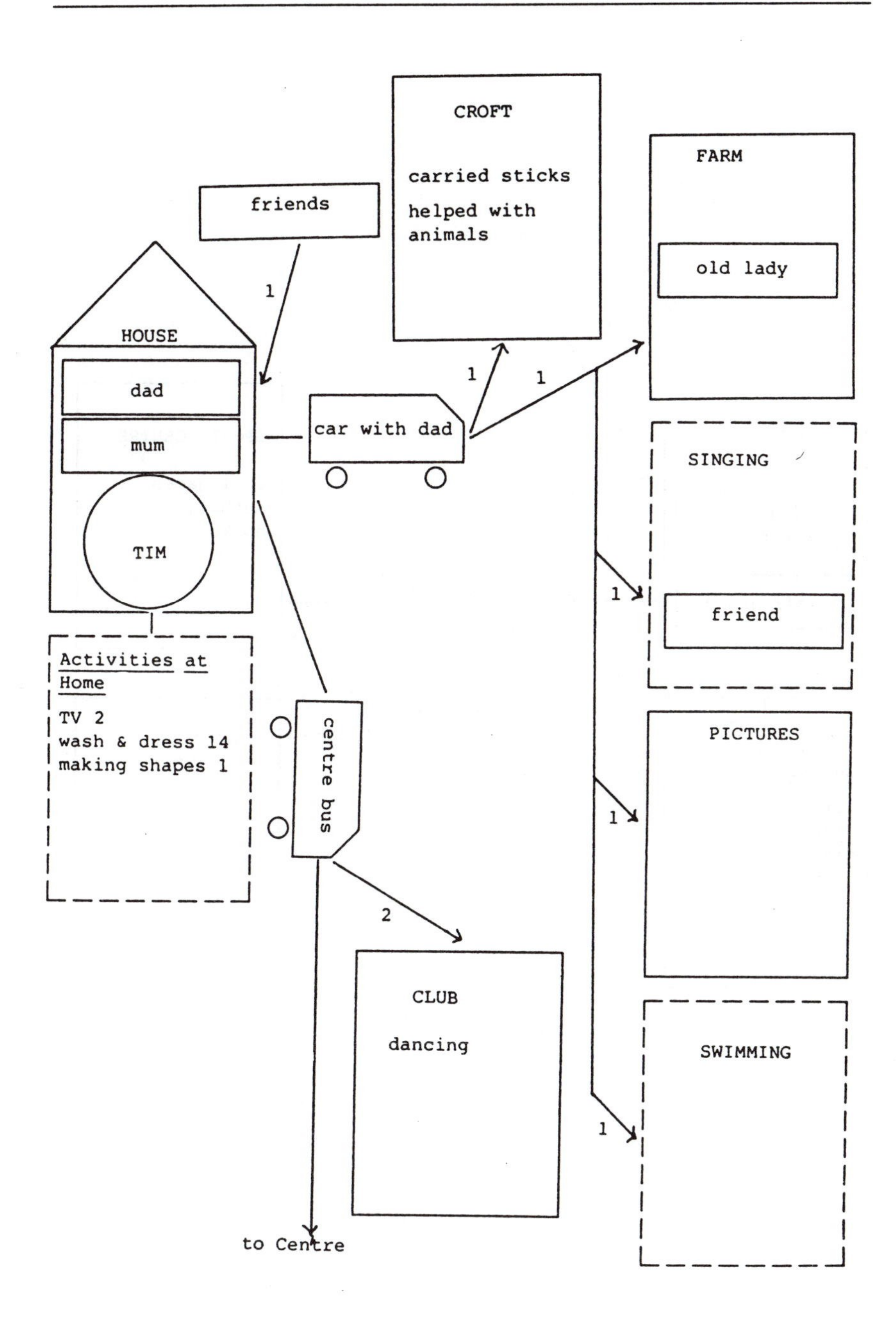

Figure 9.1 Tim – first monitored fortnight at home (1985)

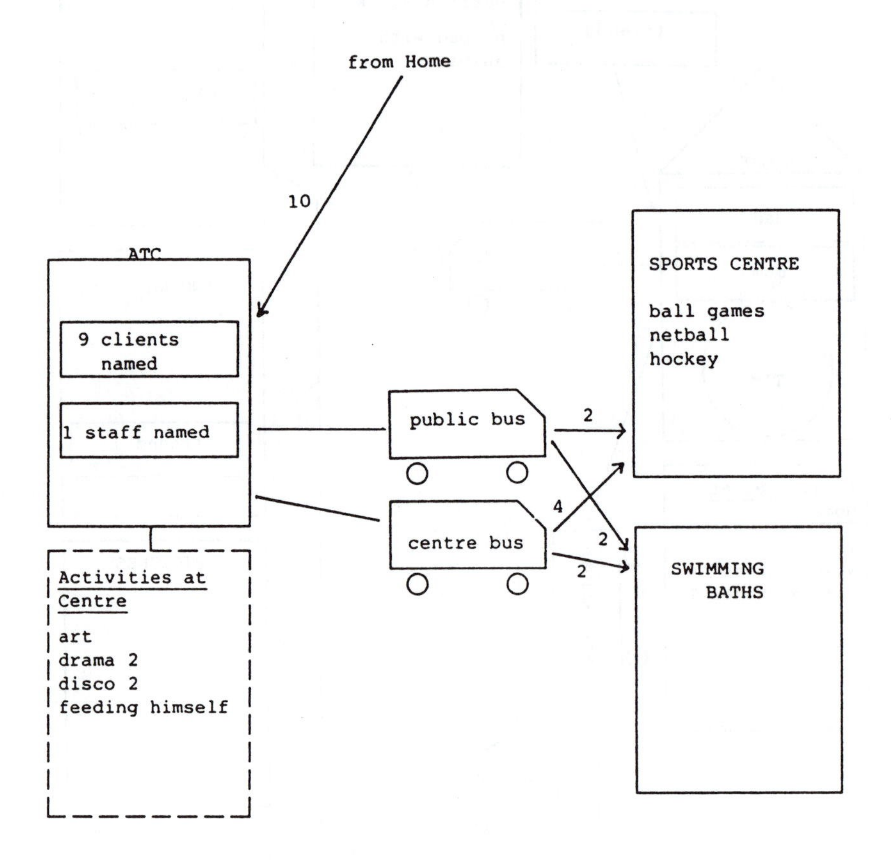

Figure 9.2 Tim – first monitored fortnight at the centre (1985)

had left – in this case to America, England and Australia. Yet the family network (see Figure 9.1) was distinctly 'embracing' rather than 'self-contained'. (For an explanation of these terms, see Chapter 5.) The father was retired and spent a lot of time with Tim, especially at weekends when the two of them went away to their country croft. Here Tim had an entirely different lifestyle.

The parents had high expectations of the day centre Tim attended. They expected intensive education to develop Tim's potential specifically, rather than generally, related to his needs. For example, one of Tim's obvious needs was to develop his communication and the parents very much regretted that a speech therapist was not available. While the general aim of social education was accepted by staff, there was more emphasis on trying to control him. He had a habit of running out of the centre to a nearby police station where he would jump on top of any stationary police cars. To stop him from doing this the staff always had to keep an eye on him and usually to hold his hand when they went anywhere.

There were different perceptions of what Tim could and could not do at home and at the centre during the first monitored fortnight.

Support Needs (First Monitored Fortnight)

Activity	*At home*	*At the centre*
Dressing	He can do everything except tie his laces. He is not good at zips but he can button his shirts	Very easily distracted. He is capable of the necessary physical movements
Washing and toilet	Washing – no problem. He has to be shaved. You have to remind him to go to the toilet	He can wash himself. We don't know about the toilet because he never goes between 9 and 4 o'clock while he is at the centre

Activity	*At home*	*At the centre*
Eating and drinking	No problems	Very fussy. He eats what he likes and has food cut up for him. He will only eat part of it. If he could, he would let you feed him
Mobility	No problems	Can never be out of sight, though physically capable. Time means nothing to him
Household tasks	Puts out knives and forks, clears dishes and puts them into sink	Just beginning to wash dishes. He lays the table with another trainee
Understanding money	No understanding	No understanding
Communication – is vocabulary greater than 50 words?	Yes – he has a good memory for places	Don't know. He can sing, with words and tune but you cannot communicate with him
Can he respond to a simple request or piece of information	Yes – but his response is slow. It may take five minutes	No – because you can't communicate with him
Comment on progress during the last year	Able to take tape out of holder in car. He fits his own seat-belt. He can give money for the toll bridge. Has become very good at closing the car door	He has learnt to to take the lid off a flask and pour his own drink; also how to cut round shapes (he used to stand looking about the room all day)

My own observation of Tim when I first met him at the centre was that he tried to communicate but could only do so by making a kind of 'quack' like a duck.

The following are the staff objectives and comments for some of the activities at this time:

Activity	*Objectives and Comments*
Visit to sports centre	Training Tim to join in relay games and ball games. Tim can concentrate for a short period at ball games but he will try not to throw to another trainee
Group work	Participation. To get Tim to use a pencil and scissors. Tim does not always understand what you want him to do. It takes time to get him interested
(Another) visit to sports centre. Ball games and relay team	To get Tim interested in throwing the ball and to throw it to one trainee. Tim cannot grasp the game he is involved in. He stands staring at the ball. He can be difficult when it suits him.
Swimming baths	To keep him interested in swimming. He is a very good swimmer. He would not come out of the water today. It ended up with one of the attendants having to go in for him
Self-help section	To get Tim involved in survival cookery. He does not have enough concentration to make a simple meal
Drama therapy	To be involved in all aspects of drama. Particularly to be stimulated by the musical work. His behaviour was good and staff expectations completely fulfilled

Activity	*Objectives and Comments*
Speech therapy (not given by a speech therapist)	To get more than a gurgle from Tim. To repeat names of shapes etc. Did not get a response. He can be a very stubborn person if he does not want to join in
Art class	To manipulate hands. Would not respond to any work today. He was in a mood
Disco	To mix and dance with other trainees
Another visit to sports centre. Ball games and catching ball	To get Tim to participate – throwing. He managed a bit better. His behaviour was good
Swimming pool	To spectate with a group of trainees. He watched the antics of other swimmers
Sports centre	To get Tim involved in group and team games. He responded very well this morning

At the bottom of one of the diary pages the staff person wrote: 'Tim is very hard to write about. He has no conversation at all. This makes communication very difficult. He will sit looking at another person or laughing when you are trying to give him some instruction.'

Tim had a more severe learning disability than most of the other clients attending this particular centre. Reflecting on this fact, and on the staff diaries for the first monitored fortnight, the researcher noted:

> Understandably, Tim's programme at the centre involves a major activity of going out to a sports centre. What he does there, however, is not very purposeful. He is physically quite capable, but tends to be engaged in childish ball games. As with some other people, I am amazed to find out he is as old as he is, as he is treated very much like a boy and acts the part.

One of the exceptions to this line of criticism would be Tim's participation in drama. Here the staff person did seem to have a clear sense of purpose and was not put off by Tim's apparent difficulty in verbal communication.

The researcher felt he did not really know Tim very well until a few months later when, during an update, he accompanied Tim on the minibus home with other trainees. Here are the researcher's notes:

> My own direct observation is that Tim has come on at the centre. He no longer quacks like a duck and instead he uses a vocabulary.
>
> At the centre I was told (by senior staff) there were difficulties in convincing staff (instructors) that they ought to scale things down and get to grips with Tim's basic personal needs. The centre recognises that Tim needs a lot of time spent on him but they don't always have the time. He is still escorted everywhere although the deputy manager told me that she is encouraging staff not to do more than gently lead him.
>
> I travelled with Tim back home on the special bus. He lives in a recessed part of a fairly busy street with a fairly large garden of grass with bushes planted between the road and his front door. The bus leaves him on the pavement and he normally waits until a parent opens the door to invite him to come in. I did not know all this but I sensed there was a routine and, therefore, waited with him on the pavement until his father duly appeared. At the time, while I was waiting he grabbed my hand and said quickly, 'My mamma'. I said, 'Yes I want to see your mother.' When I got in the house it was explained to me that his mother was away in America, visiting her daughter and Tim was trying to tell me this, i.e. that his mother was not in.
>
> I had a leisurely interview with the father with Tim sitting beside me. He listened to every word we were saying and joined in the conversation usually preceded by physical contact which he likes to make. This takes the form of taking hold of your hand or holding the top of it. Amongst other things we discussed his sexual development and education. The father said he is content to hold a girl's hand much as he is content to hold anyone's hand. He responds to sexual images

on television by making kissing sounds. I got the impression that the father was aware of the issue of sex for his son but considers that it has not arisen as a point where any particular education is required.

The most extraordinary thing I learnt and saw for myself was the extent to which Tim is independent at home. His father would never think of restraining him. He was left on his own while the father took me to my next call – he would have been away some 20 minutes. The father explained how Tim had been shown how to get in the house through the back door by himself. The first time he was being shown the father had waited out of sight in the car and watched. Tim had stood for 20 minutes on the pavement. The father then took him by the hand around the back and showed him how to undo the latchkey. From then on he could do it himself. Once in the house by himself he would turn on the television and sit down. The father would usually leave a drink out for him.

While his father was making me a cup of tea Tim sat beside me and I began drawing two sides of a triangle. I gave the piece of paper to Tim who drew a very straight line completing the triangle. I then proceeded to draw some 'e's joined together. This was because the father had told me that he used to draw long lines of 'e's. Instead, however, he made a pattern by turning the curls upwards at each end. There is nothing whatever the matter with his fine motor skills! His problem in communication is his slowness to comprehend but he does get there in the end. His vocabulary, in my presence was far greater than 50 words. He also demonstrated to me how he can sing along with his father and complete words of several songs.

The father told me more details of their visits into the country at weekends where they have a croft. Tim can ride a horse and can help in tasks like stacking logs. But he cannot be left alone there to do things by himself.

The father had been wondering if Tim would be better off at a centre which specialises in meeting the needs of people with more severe learning disabilities. We discussed the pros and cons of this. The father explained that Tim loves a routine to his life. He learns by association and once he has remembered something he retains it. Each activity is associated with a day of the week.

In general, the interview confirmed my view that the centre is not at the moment equipped to give the best service to someone like this nor am I sure that the answer is to put him in a centre of segregated severely handicapped people.

1986

There was evidence of considerable change in the staff approach to Tim during the second monitored fortnight towards the end of the research period. Moreover, a new system had been started of instructors visiting the families of clients for which they were responsible. This had occurred in Tim's case.

The following were the activities and their associated objectives during this period.

Second Monitored Fortnight

Activity	*Objectives and Comments*
Musical movement	To do exercise to movement. He takes longer than others but he is beginning to get to grips with it
Group discussion*	Just to be there. He has his turn in going round the group
Hygiene – washing hands and brushing teeth+	Helping him to do it for himself rather than someone else doing it
Language communication++	Object recognition
Games – piecing jigsaw etc.++	Recognition of pictures. Learning where things go. He is a bit slow at times but, given time,he can do these things
Assessment++	To find out what we can do for him. He is coming on by leaps and bounds but we are now using a more formal assessment

Activity	*Objectives and Comments*
Sports centre (group games)+*	To get him out of the special needs group he is normally with. To join in group games with the others
Basic cooking and setting the table	Adding to his independence inasmuch as survival cooking skills would improve. He has slight spasticity in one hand
Hair wash (hygiene)++	To see what he can do. This is vitally important for him to participate more than he does and to see what the possibilities are. He only consents to have his hair washed. He is most reluctant in other things and, for example, refuses to shave. He seems to be well looked after at home
Food and drink preparation++	Making a piece of toast. Choosing a drink for himself. Pouring out his own cup of tea

Key:
* – Major activity, i.e. at least two full days or equivalent during monitored period
** – Main activity, i.e. at least half the time during the monitored period
+ – Activity described as 'very important' by staff
++ – Activity described as 'crucially important' by staff

Swimming, it was also noted, was not included because during the summer the group had to be cancelled because of staffing problems. But, the centre staff emphasised, this would be a very important activity for him.

A comparison between Tim's support needs at home and at the centre immediately after the second monitored fortnight was as follows:

Support Needs (Second Monitored Fortnight)

Activity	*At home*	*At the centre*
Dressing	Everything except zips and laces. Otherwise support is not needed	He can dress himself but doesn't unless he is pushed into it
Wash, bath and toilet	He does not wash his hands and face – 'maybe we do too much'. He cannot brush his teeth properly. He is okay getting in and out of the bath but does not wash in the bath. Assistance is needed when his is getting dry – he would just stand. He is okay using the toilet but he still won't do it at the centre. We are going to buy him an electric toothbrush (father)	He is reluctant to ask to go to the toilet – but a staff member has taken him at tea break
Eating/drinking	No problems	He needs prodding but he can do it
Mobility	No problems	No problems
Preparation of food	He can pour out a glass of milk. He can use the toaster	He can butter sliced loaf, pour out drink. He needs support but could prepare a snack if you gave him support.
Household tasks	He can clear dishes. Maybe he has once used the vacuum cleaner. He folds his clothes	Not much information

Activity	*At home*	*At the centre*
Understanding money	No understanding	No understanding
Out and about on his own	He couldn't find his way if lost. Journeys have meaning and he can point things out	He just doesn't travel by himself
Communication and expression of choices	'Yes' in relation to food; 'no' in relation to clothing; to some extent in relation to where to go. He is better at communicating with people he knows and he now says words spontaneously	'Yes' to choices about food; 'not known' about clothing and 'no' about where to go. The better you know him the better it is. His vocabulary has improved

The following was a summary of progress made during the research period of two years, as given at home and at the centre:

Activity	*At home*	*At the centre*
Helping at home and self-management	Takes up breakfast in the morning	Improved
Recreational activities	Good at swimming – just the same	No comment
Social activities and mixing with others	At the club, he now mixes 'more than most boys I know' (father)	No comment
Communicating with others and general confidence	A wee bit. He can pick things up if he is being talked about	Improved in speech and communication

At the same time as I was obtaining the parents' views about Tim's support needs I was asking in detail about their views of the centre. First they told me that they thought the general atmosphere was good. I then asked them about specific centre aims in the form of suggesting possible aims that some centres have. The first of these was 'to help the client to learn to live more independently and to have basic survival skills'. The parents approved of this aim and agreed that it was the centre's intention to do this. They were not, however, very pleased with their success. They felt there was a lack of staff and that to do this properly Tim needed a staff client ratio of 1:1. They did not think it was appropriate for a centre to help clients to find a job but when we asked whether this aim was 'to provide activities which take the place of outside work' they acknowledged that this was a centre aim and they said, 'We tell Tim he is going to work in the morning.' Clients at this centre received £4 per week at this time which came in the form of a wage packet.

Other aims that the parents acknowledged for the centre and approved of were the provision of social activities and respite to parents. Finally, in answer to my prompt, they did not think the centre aimed 'simply to give clients something to do'.

The parents were not particularly impressed with communication between the home and the centre and they gave the example of the lack of understanding in relation to toileting. They used to go to parent meetings but the mother said she did not benefit because of a hearing problem and it was 'gabbling going on around me'. Sometimes the centre sent letters home via clients and the parents told me that Tim did not use to hand them on because he thought they might be 'a bad school report'. However, they said he now handed them over.

I then listed possible centre activities and asked for staff comments. They favoured craft work because in doing something with his hands, Tim could see the finished article. The centre had moved away from a previous emphasis on craft work and although there now still was some, it featured minimally. The parents approved of domestic work at the centre and pointed out that Tim laid the table at the centre. Similarly, they were satisfied with his going to the sports centre and were exceptionally pleased with the drama. They complained that speech therapy was 'not long enough to do him any good'.

Finally, when I asked the parents to comment on changes that had taken place in the centre during the research period when there had been improvements they said, 'Yes; I suppose so. He has definitely improved.'

Meanwhile at home, the pattern of daily living remained much as it had done during the first monitored fortnight. After the keeping of diaries was completed, I asked further questions about particular places and people that were significant. Tim was present and he and the parents had no difficulty in listing the maximum of three places and three people we allowed for. The descriptions of what we call 'relationship qualities' gave us further insight into a richness of living within Tim's home-based network which the centre still seemed unable to match or directly to contribute to. This was less true for identified 'significant places' than for the significant relationships with named people. The places singled out included the evening social club which Tim attended twice a week. The mother said 'they love to move to the music'. Swimming was also singled out and it was interesting that the pool identified was the one they attended when they were away in the country at weekends. It was, said the father, 'fun in the pool – a good carry-on'. They were 'quite energetic'. The final place chosen was the boat they went on at weekends. The father pointed out that Tim was 'a creature of habit'. They had 'friends there' and going on the boat was the most important part of this.

The boatman indeed was one of the three identified important people. I asked for each person a series of questions about particular relationship qualities. The first question was whether the person facilitated access to others. This was very much the case with the boatman. Through him they met other passengers. This was, however, confined to the holiday period.

Second, we asked about what we call 'instrumental qualities' – i.e. does the relationship offer Tim practical help? Again this very much applied to the boatman. For example, jumping in and out of the boat, the father said, helped Tim's agility. Also he went off with the boatman and they had picnics together. He got to know places – geographically. Next we asked about what we call 'sentiment qualities' – for example whether the relationship was one which offered affection, admiration, respect etc. All of these applied to the boatman. Finally, we asked about what we call 'reciprocal qualities'. This means whether the relationship gives the opportunity for

Tim to give help to others in return for the help that is given to him. The father said that having Tim on the boat made him feel that he was helping the boatman with the passengers.

The two other people named were called 'Big Harry' and 'Big Jack'. Big Harry was associated with playing the pipes. The mother gave us most of the information about him. 'He's fun,' she said. There was no particular access to others nor is he particularly helpful in a practical way. On the other hand, Tim made Harry 'feel good'. The mother thought that because Harry had no family he particularly valued the relationship. Jack was the local conservation officer in the country. He, like the boatman, was a means of introduction to others. He was particularly important to Tim because he had a speedboat and Tim loved it. 'It goes so fast,' said the mother. Again, there was a good personal relationship and a lot of admiration for 'Big Jack'.

No wonder, at least at the time when the research started, Tim spent a lot of time at the centre looking out of the window. No wonder indeed that he was attracted to police cars as the next best things to speedboats!

1995

I visited the parents who spoke of major progress Tim had made in the past few years with regard to the following:

COMMUNICATION

Tim now has quite an extensive vocabulary and can string some words together. For example, 'gone on holiday to C----.' He tends to talk about what has happened in the immediate past or what he is expecting in the immediate future. He does not recall far into the past. Improved communication has affected other aspects of daily living and, specifically, toileting. He has no difficulty in indicating when he needs the toilet or in understanding when it would be sensible to go to the toilet – for example, before going out. He now uses the toilet at the centre as well as at home. Tim's awareness and understanding of money have improved – not, it was explained in an academic sense but in practical terms when it comes to sorting money into piles for different purposes or in making purchases.

BEHAVIOUR

No longer could Tim be described as having 'challenging behaviour'. This seemed to me to reflect a greater understanding of his needs. He was settled, helpful and enjoyed his active life. As his mother put it: 'He doesn't understand dialogue – he has to have action.' This was said with reference to watching television, but it seemed to me to express how Tim responds to everyday situations.

GENERAL MATURITY

This is hard to define but the parents agreed Tim showed more sense of responsibility and awareness in his life. In the more narrow sense of sexual maturity, the parents told me Tim still showed no interest in the opposite sex. A recent development, however, had been that he sometimes sticks out his cheek for a kiss.

The parents told me more about themselves and their own ideas for the future as they become older. They are in their mid-70s and facing health issues. I asked about plans when they would be unable to look after Tim. The son who is within the UK would be sold the croft but he would not be asked to look after Tim. The father felt Tim could not be placed in accommodation locally because, so long as his parents were living at home, he would run off to be with them. I felt this was a topic which should be discussed in depth as part of the process of assessment and care management.

The manager at the centre Tim attends agreed that progress had been made with Tim and that his behaviour was no longer problematic. The centre has always, since the research started in 1984, subscribed to a goal of individualised programme planning – within staffing and other resource possibilities, including making the best of an old and ill-suited building. A new purpose-built centre, originally intended to open in 1973, was now expected to open at the end of 1995.

POINTS FOR DISCUSSION

1. Can you account for some differences in Tim's support needs as perceived at home and at the centre, especially during the first monitored fortnight? Compare this with the second monitored fortnight.

2. Tim did go out from the centre quite a lot, for example, for swimming (see Figure 9.1). Were these outings of maximum benefit to Tim? If not, how could they have been more helpful in meeting his needs?
3. There is evidence in comparing the first and second monitored fortnights that the staff moved a lot of their attention from being concerned about Tim's behaviour and controlling it to attempting to meet his specific needs. What factors contributed to this change of approach?
4. Why do you think drama is particularly important for Tim, as well as being appreciated by the parents?
5. In what ways are the parents 'supportive' or 'protective' towards Tim? Could they be less protective or more supportive than they are in any particular respects? Consider this question in relation, for example, to allowing Tim to do things for himself, to travel independently, to sex education
6. Sex education does not feature at the centre. Do you think it should? How would it be approached in the case of Tim?
7. In what ways, if at all, is Tim treated like a child rather than an adult: (a) at home and (b) at the centre?
8. Do you think this is an appropriate case for centre staff to spend time with Tim at home (as the researcher did)?
9. For whatever reason (perhaps because of the lack of opportunities at school or for other reasons) Tim appears to be a late developer. Outline your hopes for Tim's development over the next few years, after 1986. What might be the obstacles for the realisation of his potential? How would these obstacles be overcome? Answer these questions with particular reference to: (a) whether Tim could learn about money; (b) whether his communication could further improve and (c) whether he could have a greater sense of control over his life.
10. In what ways is Tim at an advantage or disadvantage in not being at a centre, or within a unit, which specialises in people with severe handicaps?

11. Do you think someone like Tim could ever attend a day centre on a part-time basis and instead pursue other activities in more normal settings? If so, how could this be brought about? Answer this question with reference both to centre activities and in working with the parents.
12. What would you see as the long-term future for Tim – looking ahead to the time perhaps when his parents are no longer able to care for him at home? In what ways was the centre beginning to prepare for this situation? Can you suggest any further activities which would help towards Tim's eventual ability to survive, and to continue to lead a rich life, without his parents?
13. In considering Tim's long-term future, how important would it be to retain his rural life contacts. How could this be achieved?

CHAPTER TEN

Day Services in Rural Areas

People living in rural areas have to travel to towns for many of the services they need – for example, major shopping, visiting the dentist, government offices. Should this apply also to day services for people with mental handicaps? Research in Scotland has revealed examples of people being bussed up to 40 miles each way over mountainous roads each day to attend a day centre.

In some cases, where there are no local services, people with handicaps stay at home. For example, I came across a situation where a mother lived alone with her daughter who had profound and multiple disabilities and who was in her mid-30s. They lived in a village about 15 miles from the nearest town. They were very attached and involved with each other and spent nearly all their days in each other's company. The daughter had never been to school and was unknown to the social services department. Probably even her existence was only known to a few people.

There are perhaps three ways in which the problem of delivering day services to people with learning disabilities has been tackled. The first is by introducing a mobile service. A proposal for a mobile resources unit was first made for the Scottish Highlands as early as 1979, but it was not taken up at that time. In the early 1980s, an experiment was launched in North Yorkshire described as 'a novel method of delivering an appropriate and viable day training service to mentally handicapped adults living in rural areas'. The idea was 'to take a service into the areas rather than transporting rurally-based clients to, or accommodating them in, towns'. A double-decker bus was converted and two areas were selected for the experiment. More recently, this idea has been linked with very small locally-based units, with 10 to 12 places each. The third approach has been to develop outreach services, in the form of a peripatetic instructor, from a town-based centre. One such scheme is described in this chapter. We shall contrast it with a second case where a complicated daily journey to a centre in a city is undertaken.

ALF

1984

When the researcher (Margaret Thomson) first visited the family, Alf was aged 38. His mother was in her 60s. Alf's father had recently died and other members of the family had left home. Alf and his mother were alone and each was very dependent on the other. The mother told the researcher, when they had got to know each other, that she had been very anxious in the beginning about being 'part of the research'. Although it had been explained that this was part of a study with a random sample the mother had imagined that it might lead to Alf being taken away from her and placed in a hostel. In the long run she recognised such a move might be necessary. Her brother had offered to take him should anything happen to her but she felt that this would not be the best solution.

Alf and his mother lived in a village some 35 miles from the nearest day centre and about 15 miles from the nearest social work office. There were local schools in the village. Alf attended a normal village school and went on to the local secondary school. The mother said it was made clear to her that his attendance was to give her a rest and not in the expectation that he would learn anything. The mother recalled that there was, however, one teacher who was keen to get involved with Alf and to teach him but a problem arose about the teacher spending so much time with him at lunch-times. The mother said this was not acceptable to the school system.

Alf received no help after school until he was aged 32 and then a group of mothers got together with help from a social worker and started an afternoon club for adults with handicaps, held in the church hall. The club was still going and Alf attended. The club received financial help from the local authority education department and it was under the umbrella of a national parents' organisation. It was, however, independent and raised a substantial proportion of its costs by local fund-raising.

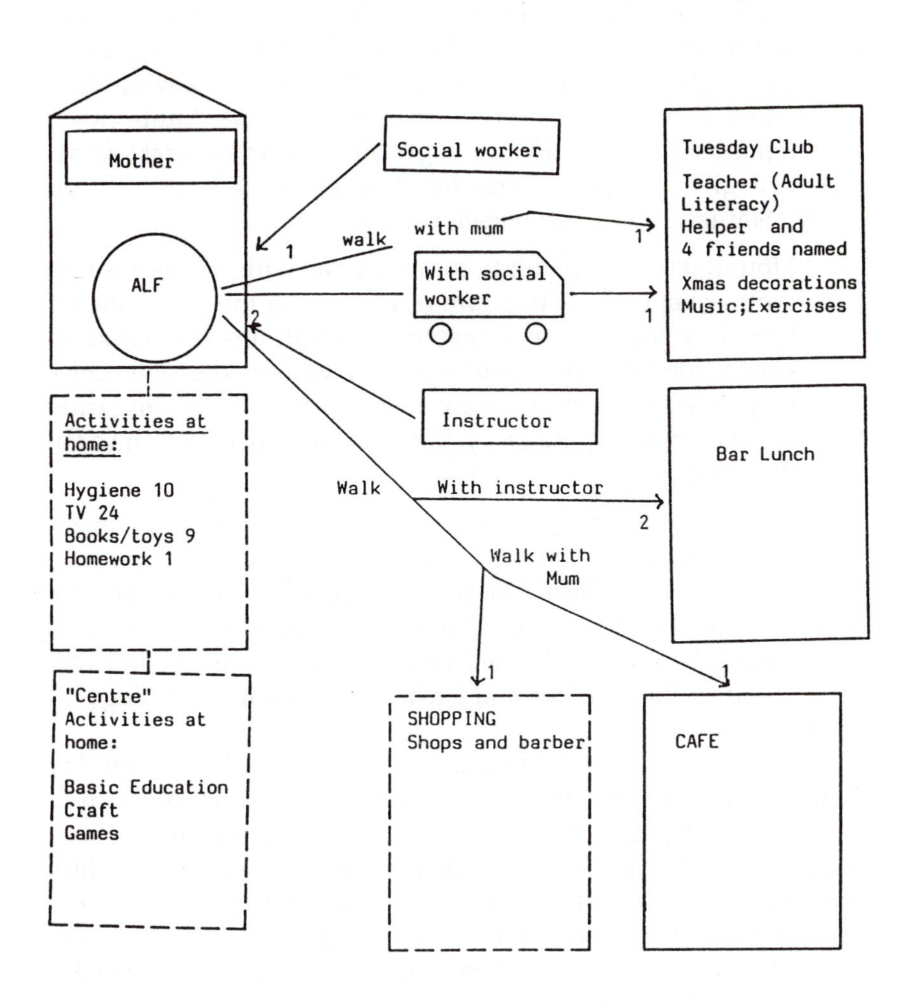

Figure 10.1 Alf – first monitored fortnight at the centre (1985)

Alf was fairly capable at self-management skills. He was able to walk although he did not in fact go further than a visit to neighbours, occasionally by himself. He needed help with shaving (from mother). Physical help was needed for bathing partly because of his weight and partly because he was afraid of certain things, including water. He could communicate although there were some difficulties. The mother said that Alf was sometimes 'quite clever with remarks' but 'it is difficult to get him to communicate sometimes. He gives up if you do not listen properly. He turns his head away.' Margaret Thomson herself recorded:

> I found it quite difficult to communicate with Alf because his mother kept prompting him or answering the questions for him. His speech is reasonable, although answers come in single words or in words which take a while to decipher. Once he gets going with the conversation, though, he can string words together quite easily and make sentences once he's got the hang of it.

A social worker was in touch with this family, visiting about every six months. Usually, according to the mother 'to give information'. Sometimes, however, he did more. During one visit during the first monitored fortnight (see Figure 10.1) the social worker came and transported Alf to his voluntary club. This was unusual and was on account of the weather and because he was in the village on other business.

Alf did not attempt the journey of 35 miles to the nearest day centre. Instead the instructor from the day centre visited him at home on a peripatetic basis. She attended for the day from about ten o'clock in the morning until three in the afternoon and took him out for a bar lunch. There was considerable emphasis on teaching during these visits. Some of the specific activities and comments recorded by the instructor during the first monitored fortnight (November 1984) were as follows:

Activity	*Comments*
Writing: shape, copying	Trying to maintain a failing skill. Slight improvement each week.
Numbers: recognition in grouping to ten	
Colours: naming	Knows only four colours consistently.
Reading: recognition of family names	Expect improvement.Each day recognises more words.
Time: hours, half hours	Struggling – excellent at hours but blocks out half hours.
Hand work: peg bag simple	Can only work with constant supervision
In and out on canvas	One-to-one guidance but is improving. Although Alf is not particularly good at hand work, he likes it and is eager to produce a finished article
Games – all educational from which great stores of information can be built up	Alert, cheeky and amazingly knowledgeable in certain areas. We have built up information on football, music, animals and television
Animal lotto	Wholehearted participation. Alf at his best. This is our usual way to end the day. Alf is the type of person who, in a crowd, would easily get overlooked but who has lots to offer when coaxed and encouraged

The instructor explained to us that the peripatetic service to Alf was first introduced in 1982:

> After many hours spent at home with a sick father (who has since died) and an anxious mother, Alf had become 'elderly' and set in his ways. As his name was on the hostel waiting list

> and he would hopefully be offered a place at the centre, it was felt that an effort to prepare him for this event would be beneficial to him. Bearing this in mind my programme was similar to what he would experience in the centre.

She also commented that during the summer 'much time is spent out of doors (something Alf did not do too much of) and we have managed to lessen greatly his numerous fears, e.g. of wind, aeroplanes, dogs and noises'.

The instructor also attended the voluntary club. During the first monitored fortnight the instructor recorded that 'because of various unforeseen reasons no helper was present so I took the club today'. She recorded that Alf was quite biddable and had a pleasant nature. 'He tries well within limited ability.' During the tea break I noted that Alf's manners were excellent but that he was reluctant to help with clearing up. There was wholehearted participation during musical exercises.

The mother saw the purposes of contact with the instructor, both at the club and at home as both educational and social. She recognised that without the contacts Alf's life would have been very restricted. She recognised that slow progress was also being made. The village had its own local shops and amenities. However, for major shopping it was necessary to travel 35 miles and the family had no car. The mother reported that it was just possible to get there and back in a day by bus.

1986

During the second monitored fortnight, 18 months later, (see Figure 10.2) there was no expedition to town. The only visit out of the house was to the weekly club. On this occasion Alf met his old social worker who, some years earlier, had been partly instrumental in starting the club. This time he also met three of the voluntary helpers as well as others attending whom he described as friends.

Daily diaries for both monitored fortnights were completed by Alf's mother. There was no real difference between the entries in 1986 and in 1984. The following are the entries for the day the past social worker came:

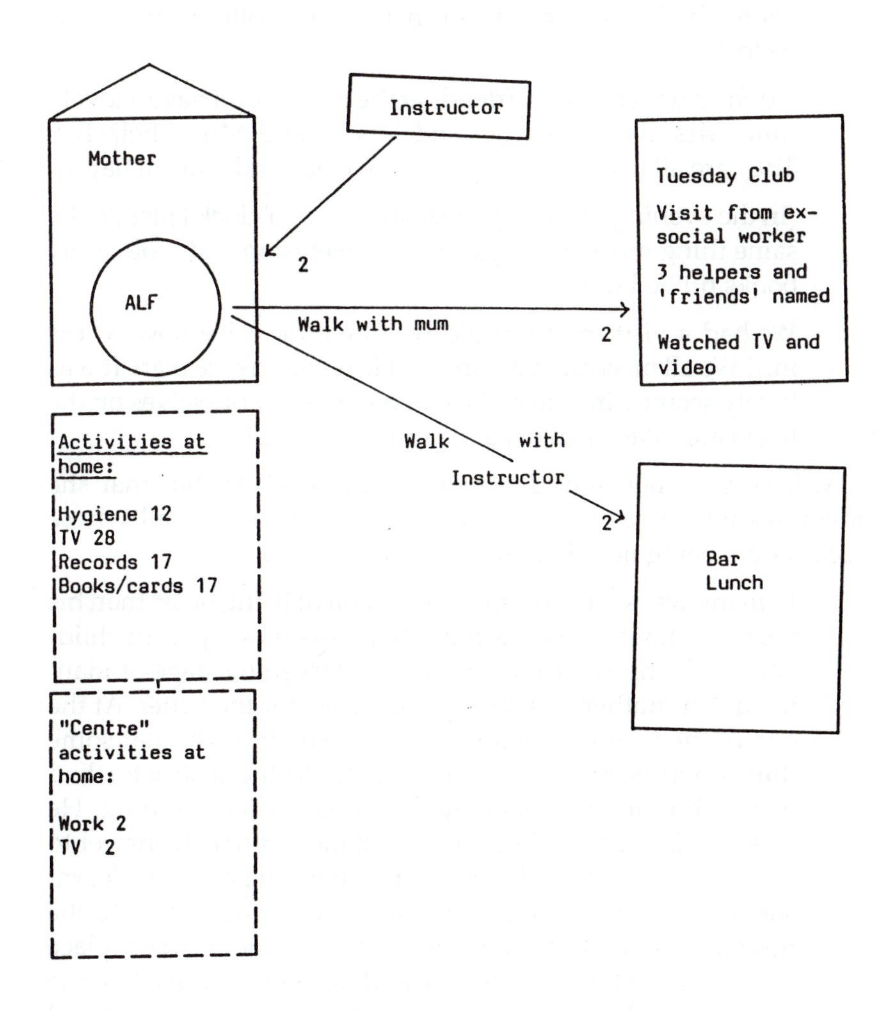

Figure 10.2 Alf – second monitored fortnight (1986)

> Got up as usual washed and dressed. Had breakfast and watched Play School on television. This is the day I go to my club so once I have my lunch mum takes me along to the church hall where my class is held. Mum collects me at four o'clock.
>
> (At the club) I meet my friends at the club. We all have a lovely time. Mrs...is our teacher and Miss... and Mrs... help her. They are all lovely people and my friends and I are all happy.
>
> (In the evening) After my meal about five o'clock I just do the same thing most evenings – watch television and look at my books till bed time.
>
> We had a visit from our old welfare officer. He now works in... We all miss him very much. He is such a nice man. It was lovely seeing him. He had a video so we saw ourselves on the television. We all enjoyed his visit very much.

It will be seen not only that mother 'mothers' Alf but that she identifies with him very closely and it is difficult to tell whose feelings are being noted in the diary, mother's or Alf's.

> In many ways Alf gave the impression of being older than his years. It almost seems as though he was moving from childhood to being elderly without the intervening stage of manhood. Yet mother was aware of changes for the better. At the end of the second monitored period, she thought that some things had been learnt. Weekly visits to the instructor had helped him to learn, she said. He was learning writing. He liked the bar lunch. He would like it more often. In answer to the specific question about whether anything had been learnt she said that Alf had greater confidence about going to the hostel. This is where he went for respite and where a place was available for him when he and his mother agree that the time for this has come. Yet even after the second monitored fortnight in answer to the question as to whether Alf had learnt to express choices the mother replied that he did not have many opportunities.

After the second round of diaries were completed, we asked Alf to name the three most important people in his life. These were (apart from his mother) the instructor, the ex-social worker and his brother. It was interesting when we went into each of these relationships to examine their qualities, that in no instance did it appear that there was any opportunity for Alf to undertake tasks to help any of them.

The mother had had various breaks from caring for Alf. On one occasion she went for a stay on the continent while Alf went to his brother's house. Alf and his mother also went together for a week's stay in a different area arranged by the weekly club and held at a university. The mother said she enjoyed it and became very aware of how much she mothers Alf. At one point during the weekend, Alf was in the queue for food. The mother said that she went to take over and get his food for him when somebody told her to leave him to get on with it himself. She said this made her realise just how much she did fuss over him.

1989

The researcher contacted the family three years later (March 1989) in preparation for this chapter.

There was little change in the situation. Alf still attended the Tuesday Club once a week and was still very enthusiastic about this. He still saw his peripatetic instructor once a week.

There were plans to increase Alf's visits to the hostel for respite and this year it was possible that he would be there for up to four weeks (as distinct from two in previous years). Alf went in to the centre party at Christmas time and this year on his birthday he especially asked to go into the centre for the day. This was arranged and he enjoyed that trip.

Alf was quite ill last year with some condition that was unidentifiable. This caused a great deal of concern both for him and for his mother. He lost two stone in weight (which he has now put back on again) and was very poorly for a while. He has now fully recovered. His mum thought that she was going to lose him.

There was very little social work involvement with Alf. It was felt by the peripatetic instructor that this was not needed. If this were the case and it was felt there was a need for other support this would immediately be initiated by the instructor. Alf's mother was still very anxious about her involvement with professionals and is really frightened that Alf may be 'taken away' if she is not doing things properly.

She has been reassured that there would be a place for Alf at the hostel in the nearst city when the time was right and that would be when his mother agreed that it was right. The researcher added: 'Alf's mum can be seen as similar to a number of elderly parents caring for middle-aged handicapped people. There is a mutual dependence on each other. Caring for Alf seems to be mother's motivation to keep going herself. She would be 'lost' without him.'

1995

Alf died in 1993. He had been suffering from Alzheimer's and his condition had deteriorated very rapidly. The centre staff said the diagnosis of Alzheimer's could have been delayed because of Alf's learning disabilities. They also said that once he was diagnosed the label 'Alzheimer's' took precedence over the label 'learning disability'. He was no longer seen as someone with a learning disability – or even as someone with Downs syndrome.

POINTS FOR DISCUSSION

1. Assess the value to Alf of:
   (a) the weekly club started through local initiative and with the help of a social worker and
   (b) the peripatetic instructor from the nearest day centre.
2. Alf himself says he would like the instructor to come more often. Yet the researcher commented that Alf probably got more attention in one day than he would get in a week were he to attend the centre full time. Discuss the benefits and cost effectiveness of:
   (a) an instructor visiting five families in the remote rural area once each day of the week and
   (b) an instructor responsible for, say, eight students attending a day service.
3. Comment on mother's attachment to Alf. How did this affect the consideration of where Alf was going to live in the future? Should the mother have been persuaded that if Alf left home it was not necessarily because of her inability to cope but because Alf could be encouraged to lead a life of

greater independence? Do you think more active steps should have been taken to encourage Alf to leave home – or do you consider that such steps should have been taken a long time ago?

4. Discuss the difficulties of transport in a rural community for someone who has no car. Although going out to the shops after a long bus journey is a major event, would there be correspondingly greater benefits from this event for Alf than if the mother had a car?
5. Comment on the role of the social worker in this case. Do social workers in rural areas have more time than their urban counterparts for such activities as escorting clients with handicaps and, in an emergency, taking over the running of a club?
6. Discuss the possible benefits Alf might have gained were he to start schooling in his middle-ages, instead of 30 years ago.
7. Discuss the consequences for Alf of his not having the opportunity to do things for others.
8. In general, Alf's social network at home could be described as very restricted or self-contained. Assess the value of the Tuesday Club and the peripatetic instructor's visits in enhancing Alf's social network. Do you think any further efforts could have been made and if so, how, to develop Alf's social network and possibly his mother's network as well?
9. Compare the signs of the onset of dementia with the characteristics of someone with Down's syndrome who has a moderate learning disability. Would early diagnosis of dementia help?

MICHAEL

1984

Michael was aged 22 when the researcher first contacted him. He lived with his mother and father, two younger brothers and one older brother. An older sister who had left home was married.

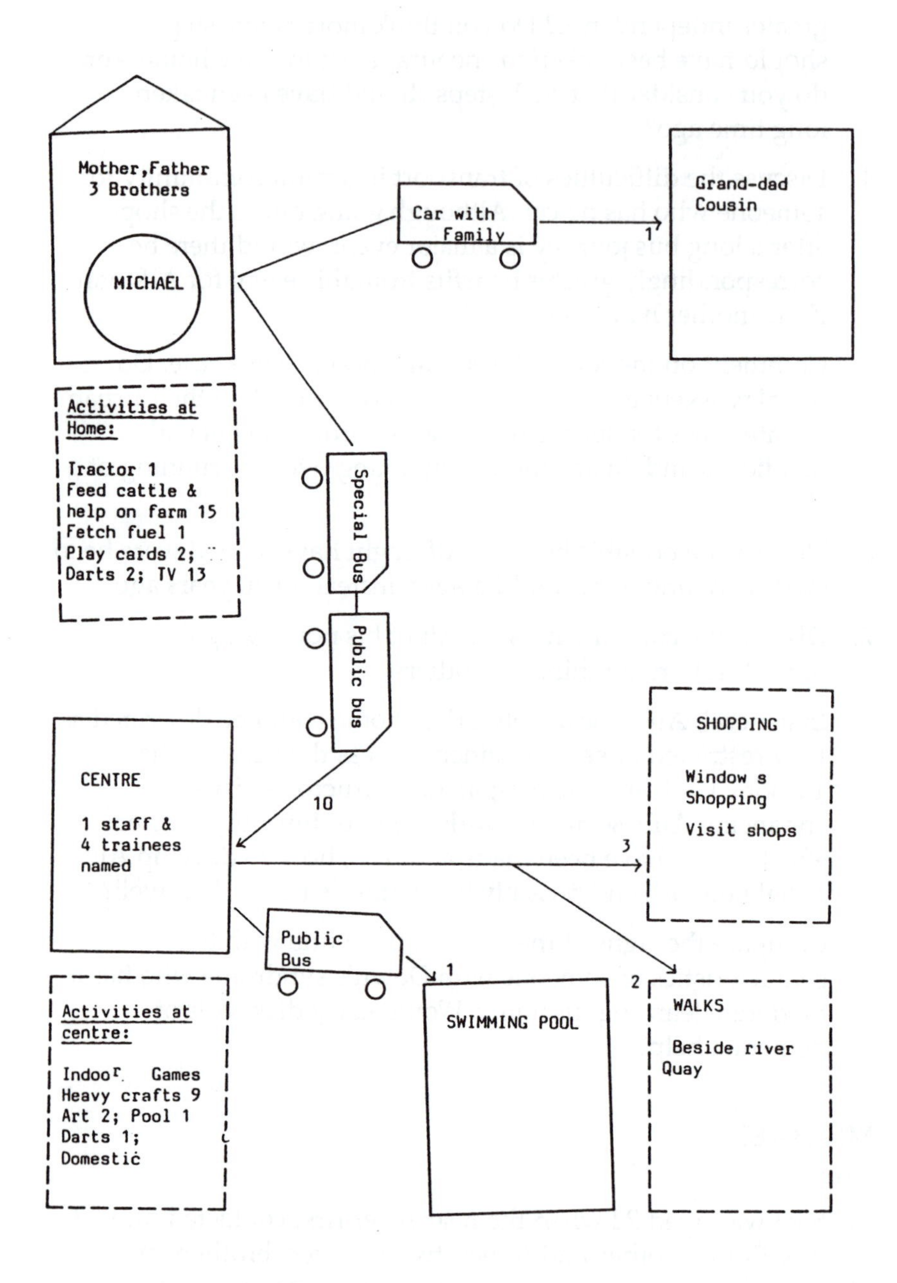

Figure 10.3 Michael – first monitored fortnight (1984)

The family lived about five miles from the nearest village in a remote part of the countryside. They occupied a tied farm cottage. They were not on the telephone. There was no public transport in the area. Michael got about by hitching a lift or walking.

Michael attended a day centre in the nearest city. He reached the centre by a combination of special bus and ordinary transport. Michael was one of the ablest trainees attending the centre. Both at home and at the centre, for both monitoring fortnights, he scored the maximum possible for our 'features of performance' assessment. This included both self-management and daily living tasks. Asked what he had learnt at the centre, he replied that he cooked his own meals. His mother said he had learnt to play snooker at the centre and his instructor said that hygiene had improved.

Michael had previously attended a special school in the city. We do not know how it was that he came to be placed in a special school or why he was considered 'backward'. Certainly there were some social problems. The mother said he was shy when he was younger but other children in the family were in trouble. There were reports of past incidents of fighting and regular social work visits took place because of supervision requirements.

The father was a farm labourer and mother did housework 'at the big house' as required. Michael's brothers were unemployed but Michael himself helped on the farm for payment on a seasonal basis. His ambition was to work full time on a farm as proper employment.

Meantime he attended the centre. The mother was pleased about this. She heard about the centre from the special school. In answer to the researcher's question about what the mother thought he would get out of the centre she replied 'to get out more'. Asked what the mother herself would get out of it she replied 'to stop worrying about finding him something to do'. She said the centre did well for Michael. 'He likes it and they are good to him. He has lots of friends there.'

The centre in question had a particular emphasis on sporting and recreational activities and Michael excelled in these. His network for the first monitored fortnight in 1984 is shown in Figure 10.3. Diaries were kept at this time with Michael by the mother at home and with an instructor at the centre. The theme in his home diary is the help he gives to others. For example:

> Gave his dad a hand to tow tractor.
> Gave his dad a hand to feed cattle.
> Gave his dad a hand while waiting on bus.
> Gave the bus driver a hand with the old people.
> Gave dad a hand again.
> Sorted his dad's cattle for him.

Apart from these kinds of entries, his main activity was watching television. He went with his mother on one occasion to visit a grandad and cousin but otherwise his whole social life outside the family derived from his attendance at the centre. It will be seen (Figure 10.3) that his network from the centre was greater than his network from home and that the centre fulfilled a compensatory social function. The following are some of the entries for his activities at the centre for the same period together with staff entries for the activities he was engaged in:

Michael's diary kept at centre	*The staff diary entries*
Worked in heavy crafts making dressing table stool. At 11.45 am went to the swimming baths. Arrived back at centre 1.15 pm. Fifteen minute lunch break (mince and potato). Went for a walk to the shops in...then played indoor games.	Woodwork till 11.30 am – making stool. Aim: to do a reasonable job. His behaviour is good and he tries to do a good job on any task given. He was then taken to the swimming baths. Aim: to swim at least one full length without a stop. In the afternoon he went window shopping. Aim: to stay together as a group and to remember some of the articles he saw when we get back to the centre. He was good all round.

For most days, entries at the centre were very similar. On one occasion, however, he was to set the table for morning tea and undertake other domestic tasks. Once he worked on an art project. Beside one activity the instructor commented: 'He can count money and write his name.' There was no record of an attempt to teach him to write more.

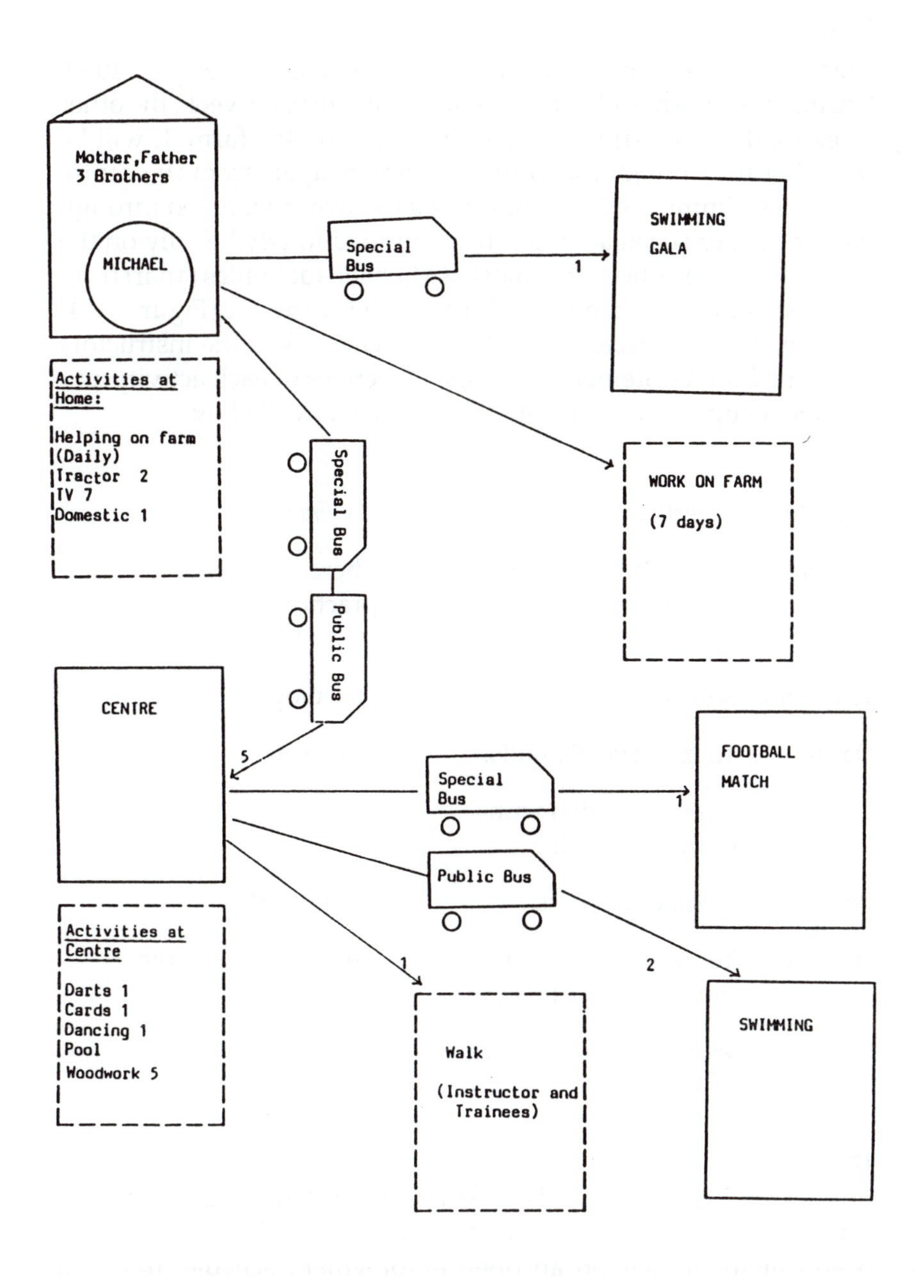

Figure 10.4 Michael – second monitored fortnight (1986)

1986

Diaries were kept again, about 18 months later (see Figure 10.4). During this time he only attended the centre for one week, the other week (and weekend) being spent working on the farm. It will be seen that the only journey out from home, apart from the centre was to a swimming gala – and this was an event arranged through the centre. For social activities he continued to rely heavily on the centre. It will be noticed that most of Michael's activities (apart from woodwork) during the second monitored fortnight (Figure 10.4) involved sport or recreation. The researcher asked the instructors concerned for a statement about the objectives of each activity and comments upon any problems. These are shown below:

Activity	*Objectives*	*Comments*
Football	Competition. He enjoys it. Exercise.	There is no place to practice near to the centre so we have totravel.
Television	Something to do.	He enjoys it.
Darts	To improve his skills.	Enjoys it.
	Basic education with number counting.	
Pool	Competitiveness.	Enjoyment.
Woodwork	To improve skills. To improve co-ordination.	The group is too big.
	Work skills experience.	

1989

The researcher was not able to re-visit the family in this case, but Michael was seen at the centre. He was back in the centre having been out for a year on an open employment scheme. It was a Manpower Services Commission scheme and unfortunately the place where Michael was working closed down at the end of a year. There are plans to try to find him alternative employment. The instructor pointed out that Michael's parents, despite the fact that they were not well off, were very open to him having a job. This was in contrast to some of the more affluent parents of trainees in the centre who were reluctant to allow the trainees to take open employment because this greatly affected their benefits.

1995

Michael is now in paid employment just outside town. He receives what is on a social services register called 'secondary support'. This means he has the services of an outreach team who pay routine six-monthly visits and offer any necessary support. In Michel's case, this was described as 'very little'. He was said to be doing 'quite well'.

POINTS FOR DISCUSSION

1. Michael appears to have a 'minimum learning disability'. What are the long-term effects of his having attended a special school for children with learning disabilities?
2. Granted that Michael attended a special school, should he, as a matter of course, have been offered a place at a day centre? What would be the alternatives today? (In answering this, bear in mind that we are talking about a rural situation).
3. Farm work is not easily available yet this is what Michael wanted to do. How feasible would it have been for Michael to have left home to seek a job elsewhere, or farm training elsewhere, if these were not available locally?
4. This family has had regular attentions from a social worker. But the social worker appears to have been concerned with supervision requirements. Is there any argument for a social worker in a family like this having a wider role? How would this conflict with the prioritisation of the social worker's tasks?
5. Michael is clearly interested in sport and sporting opportunities are available through the centre. Discuss the benefits and possible limitations of this emphasis.

6. Michael goes out shopping from the centre within the city where the centre is situated. Is this likely to be helpful to Michael: (a) in the short run and (b) in the longer term?
7. Do you think Michael would have benefited from the kind of peripatetic services one day a week which was available to Alf?
8. Comment on the problems that can arise if employment prospects compete with the family's eligibility for welfare benefits.

References and Suggestions for Further Reading

Chapman, A. and Marshall, M. (1993) *Dementia. New Skills for Social Workers*. London Jessica Kingsley Publishers.

See especially the example of 'John' in Chapter 9. Marshall, J. Stringer and A.M. Wright. *New Skills for Social Workers*.This chapter discusses both in general and specific terms issues arising from the needs of an older person with Down's syndrome with progressive dementia (Alzheimer's disease). It should be read in conjunction with Chapter 7 of *Day Serviees for People with Learning Disabilities.*

Headway National Head Injuries Association. Head Office 7, King Edward Court, King Edward Street, Nottingham. NG1 1EW.

This pressure group and educational body provides information on all aspects of the needs of people suffering from the long-term consequences of severe head injuries – for example as a consequence of road accidents, falls or in other circumstances.

Lorimer, Mrs. *et al.* (1993). *Downs Syndrome and Dementia*, Dementia Services Development Centre, University of Stirling (Stirling FK9 4LA)

Seed, P. (1988) *Day Care at the Cross Roads*. Tunbridge Wells: Costello.

A comprehensive report of the evaluation of local authority day services in Scotland, carried out 1983–6. An interim report was also produced in 1984 (Seed *et al.*) *Which Best Way*? Tunbridge Wells: Costello.

Seed, P. (1988) *Children with Profound Handicaps – Parents Views and Integration*. Falmer Press.

Report of a study of children attending (i) a small special school or (ii) partially integrated teaching in a comprehensive school setting. The study focuses on parents' views and attitudes.

Seed, P. (1990) *Introducing Network Analysis in Social Work*. London: Jessica Kingsley Publishers

A companion volume for the *Case Studies* series. This book explains the background, principles and techniques for understanding the importance of social networks.

Seed, P. and Kaye G. (1994) *Handbook for Assessing and Managing Care in the Community.* London: Jessica Kingsley Publishers.

A basic text for care managers and service providers. Provides a link between *Case Studies* and a broader framework for considering care in the community.

Seed, P and Wood, J. (1995) *Have a Good Day.* Series Editor John Harris. British Institute of Learning Disabilities. Wolverhampton Road, Kidderminster, Worcs. DY10 3PP.

A series of pamphlets providing a course of distance learning for day service staff. Complementary reading for *Case Studies.*

Seed, P. (1996) *Is Day Care Still at the Cross-Roads?* London: Jessica Kingsley Publishers.

This is an updated abridged version of *Day Care at the Cross-Roads.*

Thomson, J. University of Edinburgh Department of Education. Research in progress in Scotland. (See Tomlinson, below.)

Tomlinson, J. Chairman of the Committee on Learning Difficulties and/or Disabilities. Disability, Learning Difficulties and Further Education. Research in progress.

Index